The Guide to Translation and Localization

Preparing Products for the Global Marketplace

by

Copyright © 2002 by Lingo Systems

Copyright and Reprint Permissions: Abstracting is permitted with credit to the source. Libraries are permitted to photocopy isolated pages beyond the limits of US copyright law, for private use of their patrons. For other copying, reprint, or publication permission write to Lingo Systems, 15115 SW Sequoia Parkway, Suite 200, Portland, Oregon 97224.

Library of Congress Number 2002093513
ISBN 0-9703948-1-0

Additional Copies can be ordered from
Lingo Systems
15115 SW Sequoia Parkway
Suite 200
Portland, OR 97224
Tel: 800-878-8523
503-419-4856
Fax: 503-419-4873
www.lingosys.com
info@lingosys.com

Printed in the United States of America

Editors

John Watkins - Editor

Jeff Williams - Managing Editor

Barbara Weiss - Copy Editor

Art Director

Roger Thompson

Contributing Writers

Ting Fan, Chris van Grunsven, Willy van Grunsven, Dan Johnson, Ursula Moyer, Dan Roth, Cristina Tacconi, Cédric Vézinet. And thanks to: Donald Arney, Mercedes Edgerton, Ed Etkins, Rosemary Ferdig, Scott Fordice, Steve Heikkila, Yuka Hirota, Eric Manning, David Martin, Roopa Murthy, Ehren Schneider, Aleks Smetana, Laura Williams, and Janet Zamecki.

Trademark Information

Windows and Windows Help are trademarks of Microsoft Corporation. TRADOS Translator's Workbench for Windows is the registered trademark of TRADOS GmbH. Quark and QuarkXpress are registered trademarks of Quark, Inc. Adobe, Adobe Illustrator, Adobe Photoshop, Acrobat, FrameMaker, PageMaker, Adobe Type Manager, and PostScript are trademarks of Adobe Systems, Inc.

All other brand or product names, trademarks, service marks, and copyrights are the property of their respective owners.

Contact Information

Lingo Systems
15115 SW Sequoia Parkway, Suite 200
Portland, OR 97224
Tel: 800-878-8523
503-419-4856
Fax: 503-419-4873
www.lingosys.com
info@lingosys.com

American Translators Association
225 Reinekers Lane, Suite 590
Alexandria, VA 22314
Tel: 703-683-6100
Fax: 703-683-6122
www.atanet.org

Foreword

Thomas L. West III
President, American Translators Association

"To attract foreign customers, companies must ensure that their message is communicated clearly and convincingly in a language that customers understand."

Foreword

The past decade has seen an unprecedented revolution in international communications. A person can access the Internet at any time of the day or night and instantly communicate with someone on the other side of the world. Consumers can log onto a Web site and purchase goods and services from a company ten time zones away. And, as the world has shrunk, the need to communicate in languages other than English has grown exponentially. To attract foreign customers, companies must ensure that their message is communicated clearly and convincingly in a language that customers understand. This is where professional translators and interpreters enter the picture: translators and interpreters provide the linguistic foundation for the global marketplace.

The search for professional linguists should start with the American Translators Association (ATA). Founded in 1959 and headquartered in Washington, DC, ATA is the United States' largest association of professional translators and interpreters (with over 8,500 members in more than 60 countries). ATA's primary goals are to foster and support the professional development of translators and interpreters and to promote the translation and interpreting professions. ATA members have the opportunity to become credentialed in any of 25 different language combinations by passing one of ATA's accreditation examinations. ATA translators and interpreters are at the forefront of this new era in communication and welcome the opportunity to help global businesses succeed.

ATA is very pleased to join Lingo Systems in publishing this fourth edition of the award-winning Guide to Translation and Localization—Preparing Products for the Global Marketplace. This book provides users of translation and localization services with the information needed to have critical business and marketing materials translated and localized to effectively reach customers and suppliers around the world. This guide gives you insight into the complicated process of transferring messages across languages and cultures. More importantly, it helps you do business internationally.

Thomas L. West III
President, American Translators Association

Contents

Foreword iv

Learn about Localization 2

Learning the Lingo 4

Getting Started 8

Linguistic Quality 16

Writing for Localization 22

Translation Tools 28

Managing Document Localization Projects 32

Software and Web Site Localization: Project Management 38

Internationalization and Localization of Software Components 42

What Makes a Translator 62

Producing Quality Products for Foreign Markets 64

Same Language, Different Dialect 70

Writing and Displaying Chinese Characters 78

Case Studies 80

Translation and Localization Glossary 86

Resources 94

More Oops and Notes 98

Learn about Localization

John Watkins
Vice President, Operations

"My French bulldog, Sophie, misses our life in France. She was the belle of the ball at several well-known restaurants all over Paris. I know for a fact that she received pampered treatment, including a multi-course meal with full table service, when she disappeared into the kitchen at the chef's invitation. Unfortunately, restaurants in the US frown upon visits from dogs, even French dogs. These days the closest she gets to a restaurant is the doggy bag that comes home, wrapped as a foil swan."

Learn about Translation and Localization

This fourth edition of The Guide to Translation and Localization provides an overview for you of the many steps that you take to bring your products to the global marketplace. This book began as a means to educate our clients on the processes of translation and localization. The high demand for the first edition of our book led to the publication of the second edition. This book was updated and then published for a wider distribution. As the industry evolved, we published the award-winning third edition with LISA (the Localisation Industry Standards Association) in 2000. Once again, we bring you the latest trends in our industry with the fourth edition. It is an honor to be co-publishing this book with the ATA (the American Translators Association). The ATA is pivotal in the accreditation of linguists who provide translation and interpretation services in over 25 language pairs.

This book is a compendium of articles written by employees of Lingo Systems. We combined forces to provide guidance on each aspect of the localization industry: from procuring localization services to understanding software user interface and Web site localization. This book is intended to be fun for you, providing an overview of each aspect of the translation and localization process. To provide detailed information on all of these topics would take thousands of pages and not be particularly useful to the "newcomer" to localization. Our easy-to-read guide shows how you can successfully approach a document translation or software localization project without you having to become an expert (at least not yet!).

This book is truly a group effort: 12 people wrote sections of this edition while another 13 provided further input, comments, questions, and stories. As a result, this book is not written in "one voice" but, instead, keeps some of the character of each of the contributors. This allows you to develop a feel for the personalities involved in localization, hopefully making it more personal as you experience the diversity and creativity of an international environment. Pictures of the contributors to the book are scattered throughout the chapters to let you put a face to their names in the acknowledgement section of the book.

Each chapter of this guide stands alone, allowing you to read each section when it is needed. You may find, for example, certain chapters are relevant for your marketing staff, others for your engineering staff, and yet others for procurement. We just hope that you find them all helpful!

We provide a number of translation mistakes that have made it into the industry in our "Oops" pages. These are funny stories of how some translations have gone awry. Many of the "Oops" were provided to us by linguists around the world who have had to correct these types of mistakes made by those who did not understand the translation and localization process.

Some "Oops" have entered the realm of urban legend. You can question whether they really happened (some, in fact, may not have) but they still illustrate an important point: use professionals to manage your translation projects. How many times have you chuckled over badly translated installation instructions? Just think—would you like to have someone laughing about your product? Failing to gain market share because your product "seems" foreign is really not a laughing matter. After investing so much money and effort to develop your products, you shouldn't allow them to be downgraded in their international versions.

Enjoy your journey into the world of translation and localization. If we can be of any help to you, please just ask.

Sincerely,

John Watkins
Vice President, Operations
Lingo Systems

Learning the Lingo

There is much confusion as to how the terms "globalization," "internationalization," "localization," and "translation" should be used. These terms are thrown about in the press, by product developers, by marketing departments, by product management and by the localization vendors themselves in myriad ways. Yet understanding these terms and their corresponding processes is a critical first step in product development. You may run into people using these terms in different ways, but here is how we define them:

- **Globalization**: The process of conceptualizing your product line for the global marketplace so that it can be sold anywhere in the world with only minor revision. It is most easily thought of as your global marketing strategy and is associated with all marketing concepts (branding, establishing market share and the like). Globalization is particularly important in consumer industries such as clothing and food. Anyone can drink Coca Cola or wear Levi Strauss jeans, for example.

- **Internationalization**: The process of engineering a product so that it can be easily and efficiently localized. Engineering can take the form of something as basic as document layout, for example, to the more complex enabling of software to handle double-byte character sets. See the sections on Writing for Localization and Engineering for more details on how to internationalize your products.

- **Localization**: The process of customizing a product for consumers in a target market so that when they use it, they form the impression that it was designed by a native of their own country.

- **Translation**: The process of actually converting the written word of a source language into the written word of a target language. Translation is a crucial component of localization.

These four terms fit together as a "bull's eye" diagram. Globalization envelopes the entire concept of taking your product line global. Internationalization is performed so that the product can then be localized. Finally, translation is the "base" component of the entire process as it represents the language transformation.

There is one other term, indirectly related to this industry that you may also encounter: Interpretation: The process of converting the spoken word of a source language into the spoken word of a target language. This is done in two main ways. The first, and most impressive to watch, is simultaneous interpretation. In this process, a person is actually "thinking" in two languages at one instant (hearing the speaker in one language and immediately converting it into the target language and speaking that target language for others to hear). The more traditional interpretation practice is delayed interpretation where an entire thought is expressed by the speaker, the speaker pauses, and the interpreter converts the content for the target language speakers to hear.

From Alvaro Antunes comes: "A famous Spanish book, *El cachorro del Elefante,* was translated from Spanish into Portuguese with the name *O Cachorro do Elefante.* In Spanish, *cachorro* refers to the offspring of any mammal, but in Portuguese, it means only dog. For years, many people tried to understand why a dog would follow an elephant and what the author could possible mean by that."

Learning the Lingo

To better understand the difference between these terms, imagine that you are a product manager for a new software product that manages sales contacts. Your product development team likely assembled comments from distributors throughout the world whose customers requested new features for your, yet-to-be designed, contact management software. Your marketing department has determined the global demand for such a product and developed a global branding campaign. Your design team begins work on the look and feel of the software. Here is where internationalization comes into play. You and your team must consider the following:

- Color schemes and graphic selection that avoids offending potential customers,

- Dialog boxes wide enough to accommodate text expansion,

- Functionality that supports various date, time, and currency formats,

- Input and output functionality that supports the various character sets (including double-byte characters for the Asian market),

- Right justified text fields to prevent expanded text from overlapping the graphics, and

- A readily adaptable user interface to allow British customers to read from left to right or Arabic customers to read from right to left.

Selling your contact management software in Taiwan may require localizing the user's manual, software, help files, and the software user interface from English into Traditional Chinese. Your marketing effort may require interpreting the sales presentation in Mandarin, the language spoken in Taiwan.

Localizing your product, while sometimes challenging, pays handsome rewards. Major software and hardware manufacturers report that 60% or more of their business revenues are now earned outside the US.

Proper internationalization and localization may also lower costs. One software manufacturer found that nearly 50% of all support costs came from consumers in foreign markets who could not understand English documentation.

By offering your products around the world, in versions that appeal to each locale, your organization can increase its distribution, extend the shelf life of products, and ultimately be less dependent upon the American market.

Liv Bliss writes: "From an instructional insert provided with The Original 1862 Mouse Killer, bought years ago from an Italian company: 'When the animal is attracted under the trigger it push it up of a small amount feeling the sear which, as a cam forced from the fly, permit to the hammer to hit the nipple firing the cap.'"

Getting Started

Dan Johnson
Director, Sales and Marketing

"The road that leads into the localization industry is often paved with sacrifice, hardship and student loans. My choosing localization as a career was simple. As hundreds of languages are spoken throughout the world, our industry seems one of virtually limitless potential."

How to Begin a Localization Project

You just heard the news. Your program manager has informed you that you are going to sell the new Widget V2.0 in six European markets, and four Asian markets! To add to the good news, you are in charge of having the software drivers, marketing Web site, online documentation, Help files, and printed documentation localized prior to distribution to these markets. What do you have to do? How are you going to do it? *The Guide to Translation and Localization* has the answers to all your questions.

Your first step, after reading the *Guide*, is to define the scope of your project, regardless of its size. Once you know the project scope you can talk with your prospective localization vendor to see what they can do for you, how long it will take, and how much it will cost.

Localization is often a complex, multi-step process; to ensure a successful project, accurate and realistic decisions about the scope of your project must be made prior to project start. Given a clear understanding of where you want to go, your chances of getting there in one piece are greatly improved.

For the sake of simplicity, let's break down the localization process into manageable pieces. Once you have established your project's scope, you can then go about selecting the localization method and vendor that best suits your needs.

How much to localize

How many components of your project really need to be localized? The answer could be anything from "not much" to "all content over all product components." In many cases, timeline or budget considerations may dictate the amount of content to be localized. However, you must weigh the impact of not localizing content. In choosing NOT to localize certain products you could run the risk of offending consumers in a foreign market by not providing information in their language or, perhaps even worse, you could be restricted by customs and other regulatory agencies from distributing products that are not localized for the target market. In fact, given the current trend towards globalization of our world economy, it is prudent to consult with the appropriate authorities regarding the legal implications of not localizing some or all content.

The decision as to how many languages to translate into is frequently driven by market demand, and/or regulatory requirements. Fortunately, the more languages translated at one time, the more efficient the process is in terms of both schedule and cost perspectives. Once the localization infrastructure is established, it is just as easy to translate into one language as it is to translate into 24. Well, relatively speaking, that is.

What to localize?

You may need to localize your software user interface (UI), Help files, legal warranties, "readme" files, CD labels, CD UI, printed product documentation, and online documentation. Then there is the customer support information on your Web site and training materials used by your international office to train sales staff or even end users. Your job is further complicated by the fact that your marketing and customer support departments update the Web site weekly and you know there are product revisions every six months.

Fortunately, localization of virtually all of these components can benefit from some of the newer techniques and technologies applied to content management. Recently, tools and methodologies have been developed that allow your vendor to "recycle" translated content across many different media types. Reusing already translated material from previous localization efforts is particularly easy with regard to printed documentation, Web applications, and online documentation (such as Help files). In its simplest form, recycling text is accomplished with single-source content development; in more complex scenarios, with the development of enterprise-wide content management systems. Both cases reduce translation cost (since content is reused) and localization cost (since desktop publishing is done once for multiple output formats).

Getting Started

Putting the pieces together

Given all the various pieces involved in a product release, it is important to think about the order in which to submit them to your localization vendor. If your documentation includes 20 screen captures from the software UI, the UI needs to be localized before the documentation (or at least before the documentation is proofread so that terminology that is frozen in the UI can be propagated to the documentation and/or Help files). The difficulty that localization vendors often face is that tight timelines require that UI localization and documentation localization occur simultaneously. Because these projects frequently involve the translation of thousands of words, vendors form teams of linguists to work on both components at the same time. At some point in the schedule, after the UI is frozen, time should be allocated to allow the documentation to "catch up" so that references to buttons, menus etc. in the text of the documentation match the terminology used in the UI. Fortunately, components such as training materials and Web content can wait until the bulk of the product localization is complete—after all, end users cannot be trained until you have something for them to train on!

Timing

There are two typical approaches for global marketing: Target the US and foreign markets simultaneously or launch the English first and develop product for target markets on an "as needed" basis. Both approaches can work for you, depending upon your marketing (and market) needs.

Once your international market has been identified, there is usually a push from your marketing and sales departments to have simultaneous releases of your English and localized products.

A simultaneous release poses one main challenge to localization. To release English and localized products at the same time, localization generally begins while the English is still under development. That means that, as engineering makes changes to the UI (or the technical writers fine-tune the online Help, or any of the myriad other changes that happen during those last days of development), those changes have to be incorporated by the localization team. Obviously, this makes configuration management on the localization side more challenging and impacts the cost of the project as work "stops and starts" repeatedly to accommodate the incorporation of multiple changes.

Given these challenges, it seems natural to expect that localization is easier after the English version is released and once overseas markets request your product. On the one hand it is easier—the English content is at least stable, on the other hand your product marketing manager or sales staff develop a sudden, urgent need for the localized versions and want everything done immediately!

Your localization vendor should be experienced with both product release scenarios and should have procedures in place that support both production models. Success with either approach is a matter of planning and setting realistic expectations. If you decide on a simultaneous release, an iterative development lifecycle can help you achieve that. You provide your localization vendor with the "alpha" or "beta" version of the software and then, when you go to "functional complete," the vendor can finalize their translations. This approach means a little more work, but everything is finished at the same time. If you choose to do a delayed release, that is, localizing your components as they are needed, you can lay the groundwork with your vendor so that each component is "ready to roll" through the production process as soon as you give the go-ahead.

Once you have determined your production cycle, it is time to begin the real localization process. The first step: understanding the importance of terminology management.

It is all in the translation... From a joke sent to our office: "I was meeting a friend in a bar, and as I went in, I noticed two pretty girls looking at me. 'Nine,' I heard one whisper as I passed. Feeling pleased with myself, I swaggered over to my buddy and told him a girl had just rated me a nine out of ten. 'I don't want to ruin it for you,' he said, 'but when I walked in, they were speaking German.'"

Getting Started

Scott Fordice
Client Manager

"Growing up, I always thought I was going to play in the NBA. If only I were a foot taller and good at basketball, man, I would have been awesome! Instead I've found my happy home here at Lingo Systems. I truly enjoy helping our customers find the best way to manage their projects!"

Help me understand

Your vendor has reviewed all of your product related content for localization and has some questions. What is a Widget Whirligig? What does "Whirligig" mean? Here is where the glossary comes into play. If you are in an industry that uses highly specialized terms, you may be asked to provide your localization vendor with a list of terms and their meanings. This is a glossary. Your vendor is probably pretty smart, so if you are using standard terms from the software, automotive, medical, construction, or other traditional industry, you may not need to do anything. The vendor can create their own terminology list, instead. The major difference between a terminology list and a glossary is that a terminology list does not provide definitions of terms because everyone knows what they are. The list is distributed to the linguists working on your job to ensure translation consistency across all product components. Whether your vendor compiles a terminology list or a major glossary complete with definitions, this is time and money well spent and the payoff is consistent use of terminology from one translation project to the next.

Who does the translation? Domestic vs. overseas vendors...

You may be tempted to use your overseas office to localize your product. They speak the language, after all, so it should be easy. The temptation is even greater if you have in-country offices (such as a distributor) offering to do the translation for you.

While it is true that localizing overseas in the target country may allow better target market knowledge, it can also lead to other problems:

- Less control from headquarters,

- Risks to schedule,

- Incorrect translations due to lack of knowledge of the latest US technology, and

- Difficult communications with engineers and documentation staff due to differences in time zones, especially near the project end where rapid changes often take place.

There are successes with this model, but challenges are also common. We have heard (and seen) cases where in-country staff changed branding, modified terminology, changed corporate commitments, and removed features from the US product. Unfortunately, the US headquarters didn't know until someone translated back to English the work done by their in-country office. The parent company was shocked to see what they were selling abroad!

This is certainly an extreme example, and by no means are all overseas offices unreliable. It merely indicates the importance of knowing the special requirements and motivations of in-country representatives and vendors.

Usually a combination of both approaches is best: coordinate the localization efforts in the US to ease communication but involve your overseas office or an overseas contact in preparing terminology lists before translation and in reviewing the translation before it is delivered.

Now you have to decide whether to hire individual translators yourself or to use a full-service localization vendor to manage your localization efforts. The issues here involve time, quality, and budget (and the need for value-added services). Do you have the time and staff to hire and manage translators and determine the quality of their results? A full-service vendor can provide you with all the resources necessary for you to receive a quality translation on time and on budget, reducing your need to be involved in the day-to-day project planning.

From our office e-mails: an applicant for Chinese translation sent us a message saying, "I can be had 24 hours a day, seven days a week." Another applicant from Brazil wrote, "Thank you so much for doing this to me."

Getting Started

How much does localization cost? Getting an estimate...

Once you have located potential vendors, you must communicate your needs to them (typically to their client account manager). As you begin your discussions, the vendor representative should pose many questions to you before trying to send you an estimate of the project. Preparing your information in concise, easy to follow units makes this transfer of requirements easier. Once each potential vendor has the information they need, an estimate can be generated for you so that you can pick the lucky winner.

So now, armed with a bunch of estimates—how do you make heads or tails out of them? Comparing one bid to another is not an easy task. It is tempting to accept the offer of a few bids from different vendors and then to simply go with the lowest bid. Resist that temptation! Take the time to investigate each vendor's services thoroughly. Here is a list of questions you can use to interview a potential vendor:

- What is your company's area of specialization?
- How do you qualify your linguists?
- How will you manage my project?
- Will I receive status reports on my project?
- Who will be my primary contact during the project?
- Do you have the necessary hardware and software to efficiently handle my work?
- Have you managed projects like mine before?
- How do you assure quality?
- Will you develop and maintain a terminology list specific to my project?
- How are changes handled during the course of a project?
- What is your record for delivering on time?
- How accurate are your estimates?
- Can you provide me with references and examples of similar completed projects?

Every good localization vendor should be able to give you an accurate estimate based on a clearly defined pricing structure. The chart below is a sample pricing structure describing basic services and how they may be billed.

Project level	Price
Project management	Typically 10-15% of total costs

Documentation	Price
Translate	Per word or per page
Copy edit	Per word or per page or hour
Proofread	Per hour
Glossary/terminology development	Per hour
Desktop publishing	Per hour or per page
Output of film or RC paper, etc.	Per page
Quality assurance	Per hour
Translation memory administration	Per hour

Software, Web site, & online documentation	Price
Translation, copy edit, proof	Same as for documentation
Glossary/terminology development	Same as for documentation
Desktop publishing	Same as for documentation
Screenshots	Per screen shot or per hour
Engineering	Per hour
Functional testing	Per hour
Graphics and screen captures	Per hour

Taking the time to select a localization partner with the skills and resources to meet your needs not only saves you time and money for your current projects, but ideally, also leads to the development of a long-term partnership. The value of a long-term relationship between client and vendor cannot be overemphasized. It provides the means for your vendor to know you and your product well. The better your vendor understands you and your product line, the more smoothly the localization process can proceed, and project management and communication protocols can be fine-tuned. The long-term relationship between client and localization vendor is, ultimately, the best way to achieve quality work for each and every project.

Linguistic Quality

Ursula Moyer
Co-Owner

"Frequently my responsibilities at Lingo Systems permit me to travel the globe via cyberspace to develop and nurture linguistic resources. Less frequently, I am privileged to meet first hand with our "partners" across the nation and the continents. Besides the reward of personal connection, the opportunity to learn about cultures and history and to travel, by all means, keeps the drive alive."

Glossaries and Terminology Lists—Their Importance to Quality Translations

To achieve the highest linguistic quality possible, the localization process must include the development of three items:

- A style guideline,
- A glossary in the source language, and
- A terminology list in the target language.

While the development of these three components adds time at the beginning of a project, when done properly, they save a greater amount of time during the translation phase (ultimately enabling a much higher level of quality in the final product). Guidelines, glossaries, and/or terminology lists ensure consistency in the translation over all components of the localized product.

What are style guidelines?

Style guidelines, or style sheets, are a list of specific "rules" the linguist can follow during the translation process. They are either provided by the client or are developed by the linguist in conjunction with the client. Guidelines typically address the following issues:

- Tone of the localized documentation,
- Those terms that are translated, and those that are not,
- Rules for capitalization and accent marks,
- Translation of titles and subtitles,
- Conversion of measurements,
- Rules for spelling numbers,
- Use of abbreviations, and
- Punctuation rules.

The quality of the localized documentation is largely dependent upon the quality of the source text. For the source text to be of high quality for localization, the technical writer must be informed in advance that the documentation is to be translated. It can be beneficial to have the technical writer work with the localization vendor to ensure that the subsequent documentation is designed for a global audience. Facilitating an opportunity for discussion between the technical writer and the localization vendor means that cultural and other country-specific issues can be addressed early in the project, making the translation process more effective and efficient. Style guidelines should be developed based upon consensus among the client, the in-country evaluator and the localization vendor. Style guidelines help to create documents appropriate for the end user, and for meeting company and country standards as well as for maintaining geographic and cultural suitability.

What is a glossary?

A glossary is a list of words in the source language in which difficult or technical, product-specific terms are explained. Typically, the glossary is developed by the technical writers and software engineers working on your specific project. The glossary is then used by the linguists working on the project to ensure that the right translation is chosen for each of these specialized terms.

What is a terminology list?

A terminology list is an agreed-upon list of terms, in the target language, to be used in the localization process. It ensures:

- That the translator, copy editor, and proofreader all use the same, industry specific terminology throughout the project and over all project components,

- Consistency of abbreviations, product names, non-translated terms, and measurements,

- Consistency between country and company standards,

- Locale suitability, and

- Consensus among client, distributor, and localization provider.

Linguistic Quality

The terminology list is based on:

- The product-specific glossary developed by the technical writer of the source document,
- The already-localized user interface terminology of major software developers (e.g. Microsoft),
- Software and documentation that the client previously localized, and
- All other localized resource materials such as marketing collateral, product lists, as well as company and country standards. Company standards include part numbers, technical and product support information, warranties, license agreements, copy rights, references to other software, product names, brand names, and non-translated terms. Country standards are ways of expressing functional or cultural dictates, such as publishing standards, sorting of lists, abbreviations, time, dates, holidays, currency, and measurements.

In order to express company and country standards, while assuring consistency and accuracy between software and documentation, the terminology list must be developed before the actual translation begins.

Who establishes, updates, and validates the terminology list?

The lead linguist on your project develops the terminology list. The linguist gathers all resource materials and consults, as needed, with product developers to obtain explanations of any ambiguous terms (this may be facilitated by your localization vendor's project manager). The lead linguist also updates and validates the list systematically throughout the localization process. The terminology list is then used by each of the linguists during the translation phase. If any additions, deletions, or modification of the terminology list are suggested, they are funneled back to the lead linguist for verification.

What if the terminology list was not developed?

There are countless examples in which one term can be accurately translated several different ways. The lead linguist and the client need to agree upon which term, or terms, are appropriate given the specific circumstances under which that term appears.

Certain terms can vary depending on whether the term refers to software or hardware, or whether it is being presented in a formal, informal, or imperative context. Some terms are impossible to translate, or may need to be referred to by an abbreviation based on either the English term or the translated term. All of these situations need to be resolved by the client, the vendor, and the vendor's lead linguist before the project starts.

Examples in Spanish

- **Agreement on terminology**

  "Congratulations" can be translated correctly into *Felicitaciones* or *Enhorabuena*.

- **Local suitability**

  "Congratulations!" as well as "Welcome to" ..... is frequently used in user manuals to introduce a new product. Should the Spanish audience be addressed in this rather colloquial American way? Is there a more formal way to address the user, or should this greeting not be used at all?

- **Abbreviation**

  UK — Reino Unido (United Kingdom)
  In all cases the abbreviation is written first, with the name for which it stands written in parentheses. However, there appears to be no set standard on the placement of the translated text. Client and localization vendor need to agree if the translated text should be placed immediately after the abbreviation or after the name for which it stands.

From David Eastman: "A few years back, I submitted a translation for a business presentation to be given in Brazil. The presentation listed most of the people in the company, including the Chief Investments Officer. His name was followed by the abbreviation CIO. I just left it as it was, and I was very sorry later, because it was brought to my attention that *cio* in Portuguese means 'in heat'."

Linguistic Quality

Examples in German

- **Variation between software and hardware terminology**

  Set up is translated into *Einrichten* if the term refers to setting up the software and *Anschließen* if the term refers to setting up a peripheral device.

- **Non-translated terms**

  In projects where the documentation is translated but the user interface stays in English, there should be an agreement about whether the English term is followed by the potential localized term in parentheses or vice versa.

  Klicken Sie auf Load/Unload Panel *(Stück laden/Entfernen)*, or

  Klicken Sie auf Stück laden/Entfernen (Load/Unload Panel)

- **Style**

  Connect your printer to the computer can be translated formally into:

  Schließen Sie den Drucker an den Computer an.

  Or in imperative voice:

  Drucker an den Computer anschließen.

  Or in passive voice:

  Der Drucker muss an den Computer angeschlossen werden.

Examples in Japanese

Depending on the platform, commands and buttons are translated differently:

English	Japanese Macintosh	Japanese Windows
Save As	別名保存	名前を付けて保存
Cut	切り取り	カット
Print	印刷	プリント

Depending on the context, an English word can be translated into multiple terms in the target language:

English	Japanese
Address	アドレス、 住所
Title	題名、 タイトル、 呼称
Class	クラス、 級、 レベル、
Time	時間、 タイム

On the other hand, some multiple terms can be translated into a single term:

English	Japanese
Tall	高い
High	高い
Expensive	高い
Pretentious	高い

Some words and abbreviations, by convention, stay in English:

lpi	lines per inch
pts	points
m/cm/mm	meter/centimeter/millimeter
kg/g/mg	kilogram/gram/milligram

Conclusions

Expensive rework of the localized content can result if style guidelines, glossary, and/or a terminology list are not developed, are used too late in the project, or are used but not approved by the client's in-country representatives. With a carefully developed and managed terminology list, all project team-members work from the same resource material, thus avoiding time consuming and costly communications. Style guidelines and terminology should be based on the consensus of all parties involved: Client, in-country reviewer, distributor, localization vendor, and linguists until all are satisfied with the localization process and the groundwork for future successful work together is laid.

Writing Tips

Roger "Lefty" Thompson
Art Director / DTP Supervisor

Bats: Left

Throws: Left

Roger had another great season in 2002 as he carried Lingo Systems into contention in the World League. He hit 36 home runs, topping 30 for the 5th consecutive year, and racked up 94 RBI to go along with a .300 batting average. It was Lefty's 5th straight season with a .300 average, which is remarkable when you consider the physical demands of his position.

Writing for Localization: Advice for Technical Writers

Technical writers play a crucial role in the product development process. They are responsible for writing the content that describes your products to your end user. Technical writers develop printed documentation, online documentation (such as Help files and functional PDF files), and Web site content. They must take the technical knowledge imparted to them by product developers and present it clearly and concisely to your less technically savvy consumers. This is, as you can well imagine, not an easy task.

When taking your products to the global market place, an additional burden is placed upon your technical writers. While they are preparing documentation for your US release they must also keep in mind the requirements for simultaneous or subsequent localization. (To refresh your memory, this process of developing a product for both US and overseas markets at the same time is an internationalization step).

The sections below provide tips to help you internationalize your documents in order to make the localization process easier, cheaper, and faster.

An overview of writing tips

Layout Issues: Allow for text expansion

It is vitally important that your document's layout leaves enough room (i.e., white space) for the inevitable text expansion that occurs during the localization process. This cannot be overemphasized: formatting the translated document is far easier and more efficient when adequate space is available. Formatting costs can rise dramatically when the translated text must be laboriously manipulated to fit within a cramped space.

As a general rule of thumb, allow for 20 to 30 percent expansion of your English text when it is translated. It is best to be conservative so use the 30 percent figure whenever possible. This should result in an English source document that contains enough white space for effective localization. In technical documentation, there is a tendency to crowd pages with too much information; thus impairing the readability of the material presented. Keep in mind that extra white space makes your English version that much more readable.

In addition to allowing for text expansion, you also need to decide whether or not you want to use hyphenation in your document. The use of hyphenation affects the expansion of the translated text on a page. Non-hyphenated text generally takes up more space on a page due to the limited opportunity for convenient line breaks.

Perhaps most importantly, for technical support considerations, decide whether the translated documents should maintain the same page breaks and the same total number of pages as the English source document. It is generally easier, and therefore less expensive, if page breaks can flow during the localization process. From the perspective of customer support, however, it is often preferable for the localized manuals to match the page breaks of the English so that support personnel can easily refer to "page 37 of the manual" for solving a problem. If page break matching is desired, it is even more important to allow for that "extra white space" described above. Matching page breaks from source to target documents can add to the cost of the project, especially when the source document does not allow sufficient white space for text expansion.

When you are ready to hand off your product to a localization vendor, always provide a hard copy (or at least a PDF) with the electronic source files. This allows the vendor to double-check that the localized files match the electronic file you provided. It is all too easy to accidentally hand off the wrong revision, or version, of files for localization.

Graphic considerations: Separate text from graphics

Ideally, graphics should not contain text for the simple reason that this eliminates any need for translation in those files. If text must be associated with a graphic, try to create the text as a separate component in the page-layout application (e.g., FrameMaker, QuarkXpress) used to create the document. That is, a call out or caption for a graphic should ideally be a text block in the layout program, not an element of the graphic file. This requires less work to localize (saving you money), as the graphic text is part of the main document text and not a layer inside the graphic file. If you must include text in graphic files, remember to leave it in text form. Do not outline the text, as this makes it very difficult and time-consuming to retype and translate.

For Star Trek fans: "In the first Star Trek movie, dilithium crystals was translated into Portuguese as *cristais delirantes*, which means, literally, 'delirious crystals.'"

Writing Tips

Screen shots are a special category of graphics. By their very nature, they contain text. Translation of screen shot text is accomplished through localization of the software that was used to generate the English shots. Once the software is translated, the screen shots are regenerated. When developing application software, be aware of how the text fits in various windows. As with printed documents, avoid packing text too tightly (because it expands when the software is localized). When creating the screen shots in English, be sure to generate all of them at the same screen resolution and scale, and then save the files in the same format used by the document layout application.

Limit your font types and font faces

When selecting fonts for a new document destined for translation, remember that simpler is better. Different languages contain a multitude of accents and special characters that can become illegible if overly ornate or decorative fonts are used. The conventional combination of a standard serif font (e.g., Times) for body copy and a standard sans serif font (e.g., Helvetica) for headings is a good example of font selections that work well for translation. In general, stick to fonts that are clean and crisply drawn, avoiding fonts with exceptionally thin serifs or wispy detail.

Try to keep the total number of fonts used in the document to a manageable number—no more than three or four. Ideally, select fonts that are available on both PC and Macintosh platforms. This facilitates the easy movement of the document across platforms, if required, during localization.

Most Western European or English fonts (e.g., Helvetica and Times) contain an extended character set that provides accented letters, such as "í." However, Central European languages contain characters not included in these commonly used fonts. If a document is targeted for Central European language translation, it is important to choose fonts that have a matching "CE" version such as Helvetica CE or Times CE. Your localization vendor can help you research and locate a font set that is appropriate for the look and feel of your document.

Many other languages require special fonts that are not available as extended character sets. Several even require separate encoding. For example, Japanese, Korean, Traditional and Simplified Chinese are considered "double-byte languages." This means each written character contains two bytes (16 bits) of data instead of 1 byte (8 bits). This causes problems for applications and operating systems that do not support double-byte characters. Fortunately, standard operating systems and the applications that run on them are shifting to Unicode. Unicode supports the double-byte character sets (as well as all other character sets) directly, making the display of foreign characters much easier.

Character styles used in Western European or US English layouts do not always translate for Asian languages. In many cases they are not used at all. Character styles such as bold and italic are not always applicable to Asian type styles. Furthermore, Asian characters do not distinguish between upper- and lowercase. For design purposes, the best way to distinguish Asian characters from surrounding text is to vary the font face or weight (e.g., using a heavier version of a typeface for added emphasis). Your localization vendor should offer a variety of techniques to help keep the look and feel in your Asian product as you originally intended.

Internationalize your templates

If you use templates and associated scripts to provide a standard look and feel for your layout, it's important to consider localization issues when designing that template. Scripts that automatically capitalize titles, for example, rarely work correctly on translated content (as the capitalization rules vary by language). So keep your target languages in mind, isolating text and automated formatting in clearly identified sections of the template so that your vendors can easily find it.

From Florence Lesur: "I am an English to French translator based in Monterey, CA and I recently edited the translation for a survey posted on the Internet. There was a button, in the middle of the screen, that said *PEAU* (which means skin in French). I could not figure out why that translation was there. As I talked to the project manager, we finally figured out that the button needed to be clicked if the person who was taking the survey wanted to hide the screen very fast (the survey was about erectile dysfunction). So 'HIDE' (as in: animal skin) was translated, probably by a machine, as *PEAU*, the skin of a human."

Writing Tips

Develop a glossary

Glossaries help linguists understand any industry- or product-specific terms you are using in your writing. As you write, keep a separate list of terms that may have special meanings. Providing these terms and their definitions to your localization vendor at the beginning of the project results in a much higher quality product at the end.

Remember your international audience

When developing your content, avoid using slang terms and culturally biased graphics. Slang is difficult to translate and understand in a foreign context. Similarly, graphics can have a cultural bias that is difficult to understand. A bunny rabbit might be used in an English document to represent "fast" but for the French it looks like dinner!

Write out acronyms

When using an acronym in the source documentation, write out its meaning when it first appears in the document. When translating, the first use of the acronym is defined/translated in the target language, even if the acronym remains in its English form throughout the document.

Monitor your word count

Your cost for localization is directly related to the number of words you write: more words mean higher costs. Monitor your documentation word count by using the "Word Count" command found in your development software. Keep sentence structure and grammar simple and vocabulary choices clear.

Various output and content reuse

Many companies are making their documentation available to customers not just in a paper-based medium, but also in an electronic form, such as HTML and PDF formats. These two formats are widely used on the Internet and on electronic media (e.g., distribution CDs) because they appear virtually the same regardless of the operating system the customer uses to view them. They also have the advantage of avoiding printing and distribution charges for hard copy manuals. For complex, inter-related documents, HTML and PDF formats also offer the advantage of incorporating hypertext—clicking on a cross-reference, index, or table of contents entry that takes the user immediately to the relevant entry.

The advent of single-source and content management technologies has everyone thinking about content reuse. It is now possible to create a FrameMaker document of all your content and output printed documentation, online (HTML-based) documentation, WinHelp files and a functional PDF. Each output may use all, or a subset, of the original content. Similarly, XML-based content management systems allow you to store content nuggets in a database structure and build your deliverables from those nuggets. Both processes are great for localization, because translation only has to occur once for many outputs.

Though these methods may offer substantial savings in time, effort, and money, they also require careful preparation before starting the process. Creating modular content repositories (be they for single-source applications or complete content management systems) takes planning to create a logical structure that is easy to reference.

When generating electronic documents, you want the output style to convey the same structured sense of importance incorporated in the print document. A document that does not use style tags efficiently (for example, uses a different style tag each time, to produce exactly the same formatting attributes), requires much more time to set up than a document that uses only one style tag to represent this uniform style. Using consistent style definitions throughout your document allows both PDF bookmark data and HTML style tags to be generated in the localized files more easily.

From a recent article in *The Economist:* "One characteristic, but apocryphal, tale tells of an American military system designed to translate Russian into English, which is said to have rendered the famous Russian saying, 'The spirit is willing but the flesh is weak,' into 'The vodka is good but the meat is rotten.'"

Translation Tools

Cédric Vézinet
Engineering Lead

"Six years. It has been six years since I first started working at Lingo Systems. I had never heard about localization when I took my first step in this industry. But as you learn what it takes to deliver a great product to the global market, you cannot help being amazed. After all these years I can attest to the addictive side of the localization industry. And I am, without a doubt, a localization junkie!"

Translation Tools

Would that we had a Universal Translator: no matter what language someone uses to communicate, everyone understands (sounds like Star Trek, doesn't it?).

In fact, there are a variety of translation tools that aid the localization process. These tools assist or even automate the translation process: terminology managers, machine translation software, and computer-assisted translation tools (CAT).

Using a machine to do translation seems like a great idea. It can be cost-effective and shorten the time needed to localize a product. We have to be careful, however, before reaching conclusions about the quality and efficiency of machine translation (as compared to human translation). Translating is not simply about replacing one word with another, it's a mental and emotional process that includes feelings, cultural differences, and an understanding of the target country. These are areas in which machines are likely to never surpass human beings. Also, since language is a living thing that is constantly evolving, it is difficult to keep translation programs current. When a machine translates a document by itself, it can result in enormous misinterpretations and misunderstandings—mistakes that can cost you your reputation (not to mention money). That's why it's more efficient to rely on machines for some level of support, but not to count on them to do the entire job for you.

Let's look at each of the three categories of translation tools and see what they offer.

Terminology managers

The function of a terminology manager is to store the source terminology and the corresponding target terminology. The terminology manager either inserts the translated terms contained in its database while the linguist is working on a document, or gives a warning signal before inserting the target language term. This kind of tool is interesting, but allows only a limited degree of user flexibility and in the end is little more than an on-line dictionary. Terminology managers do work well, though, as adjuncts to CAT tools.

Computer assisted translation (CAT)

CAT tools are much more useful to linguists than terminology managers, and offer an efficient way to improve the speed and quality of translation work. These tools combine a terminology manager and a translation memory that work together.

The program stores every sentence or phrase translated by the linguist and offers the previous translation wherever that combination of words (or a similar combination) is found in the current document. The linguist can accept the previous translation or create a new one. The linguist always retains control, but the machine does what machines are good at—automating what can be automated.

You might wonder how this kind of tool helps you. Well, it is important that terminology remain consistent within your document or product as well as from one document or product to another. We have all seen user guides, software, or marketing pieces where this was not done properly and outdated terminology was used, or terms varied inappropriately from one page to another. The CAT tool changes all that. The CAT tool can analyze your electronic files and quickly reveal how much text can be leveraged; that is, how many words do not have to be translated again. You may find that you only need 75% of your new text translated. (Note: even when you use a CAT tool, it is still recommended to copyedit and proofread the entire text to assure quality.)

Once a glossary is created (the glossary can be imported directly or established throughout the translation process), the translator works on his or her word processor and the CAT tool displays the text that has previously been translated. The translator can then decide to accept the proposed translation or not. Each translated phrase is stored in the translation memory, building a dynamic library of translations for future use.

Does this make the translation process cheaper? On the first job the answer is—maybe! The reduced translation costs may be offset by the costs of CAT tool administration. If there is a great deal of repetition in the new files, however, the savings could be substantial. This is especially true if you are using single-source or content management methodologies that reuse content across variable deliverables. On subsequent versions of your material (say, going from version 1 to version 2 where you update 10% of your content), you can see very substantial savings using CAT tools. With these tools, you leverage the translations from the previous version, reducing the word count on your subsequent versions.

Even on your first job, when there is no translation memory from earlier versions, the translation is improved. The tool provides for consistency in your translation, by matching repeated text, while also creating a database of translations for your future releases. It is more time consuming (and therefore more expensive) to create a translation memory from previously translated material than to build it automatically during the translation process. By using the CAT tool from the beginning, when you upgrade or introduce a similar product the CAT tool automatically leverages the previously translated text and, in almost every case, your costs are dramatically reduced.

Translation Tools

To prepare your content for use with CAT tools, files must be converted into a compatible format. This is done in accordance with the concept of "using the right person for the right job." Linguists are paid to translate, not to engineer or to format a document. So, the files need to be in a format that is both easy for the linguist to use and compatible with the CAT tool. Typically, this format is RTF (the standard rich text format). So, no matter what your source content format (such as XML, FrameMaker, .RC files or the like), the file preparation step occurs to convert that content into a tagged version of an RTF file.

With this file conversion process, it is worth your time to prepare "clean" source files (no matter what the format). If you have unnecessary formatting tags, inconsistent document formatting, or other problems in your source material, your localization vendor has to spend time cleaning the files so that they are suitable for the translation process. For example, when using the Translator's Workbench for Windows with FrameMaker documents, the necessary conversion process from MIF (Maker Interchange Format) files to RTF files can only take place if the hyphenation is turned off and if there are no change bars in the files. The use of soft returns in the middle of sentences is a problem as well since they are converted as tags and will cut off sentences in the RTF files, making the translation process much more difficult. Coordinate with your vendor's Translation Tools Manager in order to know what you can do to deliver your files in the best possible shape. This means you don't have to pay the translation agency for basic source document formatting that can easily be done in-house by you or your desktop publishing experts.

The ideal situation is to finalize the source document once you have consulted your vendor to learn the specifics of file formats and document formatting requirements. The bottom line is to save money (as always) and to avoid costly localization problems while achieving the highest quality translation possible.

Machine translation tools

Machine translation tools (MTs), on the other hand, take care of the whole translation process for you. MTs are based on advanced computational linguistic analysis. They represent the closest thing we have to that Universal Translator. While MT provides a needed function in the localization industry, it is not generally suitable for typical localization applications.

In order to have the MT translate a document, it must be free of typographic errors, misspelled words, and grammatical errors. Those factors influence the way the machine understands the text and translates it. Yes, those machines are pretty smart, but apparently not smart enough to cope with mistakes. In fairness though, these tools are useful for someone who needs to understand the general meaning of a document without caring about having a high-quality translation. This type of translation is now referred to as a "gist" translation—it gives you the gist of the meaning.

To bring MTs to the next level of application (beyond "gist" translation) requires more sophisticated content development techniques. In addition to being free of errors, the source material is written in a type of stylistic English that uses relatively simple sentence constructs. This "constrained English" is then easier to process given the linguistic rules in the MT system. Using constrained English, along with an industry- and product-specific terminology list, can generate some very good machine translated content. This machine translated content can then be copy edited and/or proofread by a native speaker to polish the work.

Although experienced translators can use MT tools very effectively, the use of fully automatic MTs by an inexperienced person (one who is not a professional translator) can lead to situations where the quality of the translation is laughable at best, insulting at worst. Here are some examples (Spanish to English) of what can happen when a professional translator, fully apprised of the limitations of machine translation, is not involved in the translation process.

Original English	Human Translated Spanish	Machine Translation of Spanish in English
Using the Wand Pen... sweep the pen tip quickly and smoothly across the entire bar code. A very light touch is all you need.	Usar la Vara Escribe... Barrida la pluma ladea rápidamente y fácilmente por el entero obstruye codificatión. Un muy toque de la luz es todo lo que requiere.	To use the twig writes swept the pen tilts quickly and easily by the entire obstructs codification. A very touch of the light is all it requires.

While these translation examples are somewhat humorous, it is important to realize the repercussions. In the wrong hands, machine translation can be catastrophic for your image.

To effectively use machine translation in your localization process, you must plan for it from the beginning and expend the resources necessary to have the best quality source materials and translation tools. The English content must be written to exacting standards; no fancy wording is allowed! Most organizations that use machine translation successfully report the development of "stylized English" that must be used by the technical writers in generating content. Using stylized English allows the machine translation developers to establish customized databases and grammar rules for each target language, improving the quality of the resulting translation. Even so, the machine-translated text must still be reviewed by human linguists to ensure quality.

Project Management

Yuka Hirota
Quality Assurance

"Japan is a small country and everyone is sitting on everyone else's lap. Here in the US everyone has a lot of space to themselves. Sometimes I think they have too much space. That is why I like my tidy office here at Lingo Systems. I have my own desk, my own phone and my own red pen to mark corrections. What else do I need? On any given day the Quality Assurance department might review documents from China, Germany, Brazil, Italy, Russia, France, and my native Japan. And I am lucky to work with an eclectic group of people from all over the world. That's what I call armchair traveling."

Managing Document Localization Projects

Documentation used to be simple: it was a printed operator manual or service manual or user guide that sat on the shelf. Today, documentation is a complex series of interconnected products that work together to ensure that the target audience receives the message. Documentation may consist of printed and online versions of the document content (often with shared or replicated content), as well as summary "posters" and "quick help" guides for end users with short attention spans. And then there is documentation written for internal corporate use. Documentation designed for internal use may follow different rules. Your multinational company might be implementing a new Enterprise Resource Program that links your accounting and production facilities in three countries. As a result, you have 8,000 training slides and support documents for training the new system users in Belgium and China. Localizing these documents, typically, does not require the same high-level consumer quality as a tractor operating manual or a blood glucose monitoring device.

To begin the localization of your documentation, you have to consider a few basic points:

- The purpose of the documentation (review, educational, support, background information),

- The level of localization that meets your needs (consumer quality or draft quality to get the "gist" of the document or somewhere in between), and

- Your intended audience (novice, sophisticated, experienced, educated, conservative).

Your localization provider is poised to help you assess these issues so that the localized documentation meets your needs. Once these parameters are defined, the project manager is off and running to provide the localized documents.

Getting started

When beginning a documentation project it is very important to agree on the project scope with your localization provider. Establishing a clear scope helps avoid problems later in the project, especially those of unfulfilled expectations. Your localization provider should ask you questions that range from basic formatting issues to more complicated linguistic issues. The more questions you can answer, the smoother the localization process is for you and your provider. Whenever possible, begin planning your localization project as early in the development cycle as possible. Projects that are rushed into production run the risk of scope creep. Planning helps preserve your timeline, ensure a higher quality end product with fewer errors, and avoids the chance of incurring costly rush charges.

If you are new to localization, you may wish to consider internationalization and localization consulting before you actually release your documents to localization. Internationalization helps you to consider localization issues before localization begins. Issues such as writing style, page formatting, encoding for HTML, content database interfaces, and the like can all affect how localization proceeds. By understanding the implications of your choices during the development stage, you can avoid unnecessary complications and increased costs during localization. For some pointers on preparing your documentation for localization, please see the section on "Writing for Localization."

Terminology

Industries, companies, and products all have specialized terms. These terms are key concepts that provide the backbone to the translation. You should create a list of these terms (referred to as a terminology list or a glossary if definitions are also provided) for your localization team. If you are stumped at preparing a terminology list, your localization provider can do this for you by reviewing all your content and "plucking" out terms that seem industry, company, or product specific.

The first step in localization is to translate your specific terminology list. Actually, this might be the second step if you have not created a terminology list! This translated terminology list provides a ready reference for every linguist working on your project to ensure that the same concepts are translated the same way each time.

Project Management

The terminology list may be augmented by any previously translated material that you have. Consistency is nearly the "holy grail" of localization. As language is an art, and many artists may work on your product, saying things the same way each time is a sign of high product quality. Looking at previously translated material and reference terminology lists makes this possible. Whenever possible, you want to have your terminology list finalized before work begins on the project content. If you can, have an in-country contact within your company review the terminology list. Discuss the review process and standards with your localization provider - and communicate those standards and expectations to the reviewer. This helps make the process progress smoothly.

If your documentation supports a software application, it is important for your localization vendor to translate these components first, so that terms in your user interface are correctly referenced in your documentation (in fact many terms from the user interface are incorporated into the terminology list).

Formatting for print and online documents

Today, formatting a document involves issues from page layout considerations for printed documents to screen layout for online documentation, Help files, and Web pages. As a result, formatting is not always done by desktop publishing experts—you may need experts in help file engineering or HTML layout to give your localized documents that professional look.

Most printed documentation today requires page layout expertise to smoothly integrate text flow, graphics, and images. For many languages, more words are necessary in the translated text than in the original English text. This is referred to as text expansion. A complete page of English text expands to 1.3 pages (or even more) in German. Due to text expansion of many translated languages, your localization provider needs to know if it is necessary for the localized document to match the page breaks in the source document (this is called page matching).

Online documentation avoids some of these pitfalls of text expansion and page matching, but introduces some other special considerations at the same time. If your documentation is displayed on a computer screen in HTML, WinHELP, PDF, or some other online format, scroll bars eliminate the concern of text expansion. The user can simply scroll farther down on the page to read the "expanded" text. However, other page elements like graphics and buttons that contain text may need to be resized to fit the longer localized terms. Similarly, on-line forms must also be resized to accommodate text expansion and engineered to support the user entering special characters, international style phone numbers, and foreign addresses (along with any other special requirements of your international users). Your forms should also be adjusted to cope with user created text expansion.

Finally, while online display simplifies page layout, considerations for the engineering of the product must be taken into account. With online displays, you must verify that the content displays correctly on the operating systems and typical viewing applications available in your target market. To ensure this, your localization provider performs localization testing (also referred to as functional testing) on the online documents. Be sure you discuss the specific engineering testing requirements with your localization vendor so that you are both clear on testing expectations.

Communication

Communication is the cornerstone of successful project management in any field. In translation and localization work, the project manager must effectively communicate your needs to the translation and localization team working on your project and similarly communicate issues the localization team has back to you and your colleagues.

Typically, representatives from both sides (the client and the provider) work together throughout the project, with the localization project manager (PM) serving as the main conduit of communication. A typical localization team includes a key contact person for the client, an in-country reviewer provided by the client (often someone from the target country serving as a distributor or collaborator of the product who can offer advice on the terminology and style for your target countries), and a technical expert who can answer questions about the technical specifications discussed in your source document. On the localization provider side, the PM coordinates project resources, including engineers, desktop publishers, quality assurance specialists, and linguists. Any issues encountered by these resources are funneled back to the client by PM for resolution.

It is important to clearly communicate your expected delivery dates, delivery format, and media at the beginning of the project. Similarly, your localization team should communicate expected delivery dates and any issues that need to be resolved back to you. Typically, the localization provider determines the timeline at the project start, based upon the availability of linguistic and technical resources. The PM confirms the anticipated delivery date with you so that all expectations are met.

Project Management

Eric Manning
Project Manager

"I had never even heard of localization when I moved to Portland three years ago from Washington, DC. I left that 'international' city to escape the bureaucrats; now I work daily with people living in Beijing, Helsinki, Buenos Aires, and Paris. It's invigorating to be a part of this global, 'always-awake' community—and who'd have thought my 3 years of high school Latin would ever come in handy? (Actually, it doesn't, except to amuse our linguists.)"

Remember, you know your product better than anyone else does, and your localization vendor appreciates receiving as much support information as possible ahead of time. This could include anything that may be helpful for translators to understand your product better (such as previous glossaries, terminology lists, or product descriptions).

Your localization project manager should establish a clear communication protocol with you. This allows all questions or issues that arise during the project to be dealt with in an effective and timely manner. In the event that you are away from your office while your document is being localized, always bring your replacement up to speed on the project's progress and be sure to let your PM know whom to contact with questions while you are away.

Beyond the fruitful transfer of information between you and your project manager, clearly defined status reports should be given to you by your localization provider. Typically, status reports are provided weekly, in written form, outlining the progress of your project, summarizing pending and resolved issues, and tracking deliveries. While some localization providers are able to provide this information through a user interface on a Web site, you can, and should, request summary reports that meet your specific needs.

During the project

Your localization project manager should keep you informed of the status of your project via e-mail, phone, or fax based on your requested method and frequency.

Although the majority of projects involve localizing a document that has already been completed in English, you may need to change or modify the source document after localization begins. Frequent changes during the course of a project can become expensive and severely impact the original timeline. For example, if you need a very quick turnaround time for your changes, you might incur rush charges. Communicate clearly what, where, and when these changes are to be made so that your PM can quickly incorporate them into the final product. Either you or your localization provider can choose to maintain the "master English" copy, keeping it up-to-date with all the changes, allowing for the final, localized versions to be checked against the latest English version.

Changes to the original project scope may cause an increase in localization costs and/or a delay in delivery. Your localization provider should submit an estimate for each new change, subject to your approval, that addresses both additional costs and any delivery date adjustments that may be necessary prior to incorporating the changes.

Completing the project

Once the final versions of your documents are completed, they are delivered to you by the localization provider. Typically, delivery is performed electronically (either via FTP or e-mail), though special delivery requirements could include CD-ROM, print film, or other format. You should always review your delivery to ensure that your provider addressed all your needs while performing the localization.

Feedback to the localization provider is an important closing step to the project. By communicating to your provider the positive (and negative) events throughout the life of the project, process improvements can be made that help your localization provider offer more effective services to you and other clients in the future. Your localization provider should solicit your comments and feedback in a standardized manner. Your input is essential to your provider's efforts to improve service and performance on future projects. Offer a candid critique of areas where your provider failed to meet your expectations and praise for tasks well done.

Another anecdote from Michèle Landis: "An American, looking for 'natural' food, comes into a bio-food store and asks for a jar of jam without preservatives, literally translated as *un pot de confiture sans préservatifs*. To fully appreciate this you have to know that, in France, *préservatifs* refers to some contraceptive devices!"

Project Management

Barb Weiss
Project Manager

Two truths and a lie:
1) Barbara once harbored such a strong loathing of canned red beets that, as a young girl, she'd secretly spit them out in her napkin and feed them to the dog under the table. She was never caught until one day when her mother wondered why the dog's tongue was red. 2) Barbara once traveled to Guatemala and climbed up the side of a live, spewing volcano, just to see what was on the inside. 3) In fulfillment of a life long love affair with all things hot and loud, Barbara used to work summers as a pyrotechnic lighting fireworks displays. She has now found her true calling standing in front of a fiery hole with a 2000 degree ball of hot glass twirling on the end of a steel rod.

Localization for Software and Web Sites: The Importance of Project Management

What is it?

Localizing software and Web sites involves the translation of application software, online documentation (such as Help files and Web pages), and related applications from a source language into a target language. For example you want to translate your marketing Web site for widgets from English into French, Italian, Spanish, German, and Japanese, so that you can market the product in the country of the target language (thereby increasing your widget sales). Software localization means that kids in France grow up using the "Enregistrer sous" command while your kids in the US hit the "Save As" command. Have you ever seen the Arabic version of Microsoft Word or Finnish Netscape? How about on-screen instructions for a Hewlett-Packard deskjet printer in Thai? These examples show just how successful you can be in giving your software products the look and feel of having been developed in and for the target market.

Why is it demanding?
Large word counts, many files

One of the major differences between software/Web site localization and document localization is that, typically, electronic content (be it in software, online documentation, Web sites, or Help systems) often has a large volume of words, scattered through many files. Text for translation can be found in source code, resource files, HTML files, script files, and Help content (such as RTF) files that your team of software engineers and technical writers has undoubtedly spent a large amount of time writing. To actually see all this text, the software has to be "reassembled" before everything can be displayed correctly on the screen. A typical marketing and sales Web site may contain hundreds of HTML files, integrated with thousands of records in a database, not to mention programming script, all of which make up the final product. Translation must happen quickly and terminology must be consistently implemented across all these components and their related file types. No wonder it gets complicated!

Timeframe

As is often the case, you may hope to have your software and Web sites released simultaneously in multiple languages. If you are even more ambitious, you may wish to release the foreign language version at the same time as the original English version because your Korean customers may not want to wait another six months before they can learn about the Korean version of your product. A simultaneous product release requires that localization begins while the source content is still being finalized. Any changes to the software, such as how and when certain commands are executed, terminology of commands, button names, or warning messages, must then be immediately incorporated into localized versions as they are being translated. The translation work can usually be completed within several weeks after the US program is finalized. The kind of timeframe required of a simultaneous release is, usually, very tight. The scenario is comparable to sending twenty workers to replace the roof of your five-bedroom house while simultaneously replacing the foundation.

Why is project management important?

Executing a simultaneous release of a product with many components into multiple languages is a complicated task requiring expert project management from both you and your localization vendor. To illustrate the complexity of localization, consider this example: it takes four hours for grandma to knit a vest. So how many grandmas would it take to have four vests knitted in thirty minutes? Though professional linguists/engineers can work in a more organized way than granny does, the simple logistics of which vest should be knitted first, who works on the heart-shaped pockets, where the yellow yarns should be stored, and so on, illustrates the need for effective management and monitoring for a successful vest-knitting venture. In a localization project, the project manager (PM) coordinates and schedules project resources, monitors progress, troubleshoots issues, and provides necessary information for all personnel to successfully complete the project on time.

At a car rental agency in Japan: "When passenger of foot heave in sight, tootle the horn. Trumpet him melodiously at first, but if he still obstacles your passage then tootle him with vigor."

Project Management

Dan Roth
Senior Project Manager

Born September 13, 1916, Llandaff, South Wales. The son of an adventurous shipbroker, he was an energetic and mischievous child and from an early age proved adept at finding trouble. His very earliest memory was of pedaling to school at breakneck speed on his orange tricycle, his two sisters struggling to keep up as he whizzed around curves on two wheels. No, wait. That's Roald Dahl. But he does like bikes.

Project Management Components of a Successful Localization Project

Starting a project

- **Developing project specifications:** The PM organizes resources and plans the schedule according to client requirements. It is important that the PM have a clear understanding of your expectations, especially with regard to the format of your deliverables, whether certain Quality Assurance (QA) steps/tests should be performed, what deadlines need to be met, and so on.

- **Specifying the time to freeze the software (or Web site, or online documentation):** In a simultaneous release project, it is very helpful for your localization vendor to know when you are "freezing" development for the release version. This is especially challenging for Web-based projects as content is always evolving.

- **Specifying the build environment:** The build environment must be specified. Sometimes, it takes localization engineers hours to determine the correct build environment which is then reflected in your invoice. It is much better to provide a "localization kit" that clearly explains your build environment so that your vendor can compile effectively.

- **Establishing communication lines:** It is essential to work with your localization vendor to establish a communication protocol. Indicate who should be contacted with technical questions or issues, if they arise, and how this communication should take place (telephone, e-mail, etc.). Often, it is a good idea for the localization engineers to communicate directly with your programmers and testers.

During a project

- **Version control:** When translation occurs in parallel to software development, it is essential to keep track of the latest software version. Configuration management, both your own and that of your vendor, ensures that the right files are delivered to you at the end of the project.

- **Change orders:** While your vendor should be able to accommodate needed changes, keep in mind that multiple changes can be costly and, sometimes cause your project to go over budget, not to mention the impact multiple changes can have on the project schedule. Try to keep changes to a minimum.

- **Tracking changes:** Any changes to functionality and/or terminology should be incorporated into localized versions. It is important for your localization vendor's PMs to have a clear idea of what changed, how, and when. Those changes should be echoed back to you so that you can verify that they are understood and ultimately implemented correctly.

- **Solving issues:** Be prepared to discuss issues concerning your project as they arise. If your vendor needs your input, it could delay the project if you cannot be reached.

At project end

It is very helpful for your localization vendor to receive your post-project comments. How well did the vendor serve you? Are there specific areas in which your vendor can improve for the next project? What went exceptionally well during the project? Constructive response from you, the client, will help your vendor provide the best, most customized service for you on your next project.

From Michèle Landis: "When drawing money from an ATM in the little town where I live when in France, I read the instructions in English. They were fine until the end when the grateful machine displayed: 'Thank you for your custom' after I had taken my money. The French was *Merci de votre visite,* which would have been better translated 'Thank you for calling.'"

Software Localization

Chris van Grunsven
Localization Engineer

"A native Oregonian for 29 years, it's my job to keep track of local to-do's, and bring the home brew for late night work parties. Every now and then they even let me do some software projects."

Internationalization and Localization of Software Components

Bringing your software product to an international market is a two-part process: first the software must be internationalized and then it is localized. Software internationalization involves the preparation of your original source code for the localization process. Software localization transforms the English (source language) software into one or more target languages, giving the product the look and feel of having been created in the target country. (Internationalization is sometimes referred to by the abbreviation I18N—I followed by 18 letters, then the letter N. Localization is often abbreviated as L10N.)

- Software user interface (UI),

- Online documentation (such as Help files and functional PDF files), and,

- Web sites (and their associated HTML/SGML pages, scripts, and applets).

Software internationalization

Software internationalization is the process of developing software products (or re-engineering already developed software) with the global market in mind. There are several issues to consider before the localization of software products, in any of the three categories, can begin. Each subsection below gives tips and pointers to help you through the internationalization process.

Separate source code from the user interface

At the software design and development level, certain principles help to determine how easily software can be localized and translated. The most basic advice is to separate the text that is going to be displayed on the screen from the core program code. Although it is certainly easier to write code with error messages and button labels placed near where they are used in the program's code, this means that the translator needs access to your code to get to the strings that are to be translated. No doubt you are familiar with the maxim "always use the right person for the right job." Translators, while experts at speaking and writing a foreign language, are not necessarily software engineers. By separating the text from the code, you limit the translator's access to the actual code. If they do not have access to your code core, they cannot break it! Two common ways of separating text from code are through the use of header files and resource files.

Header files

Header files are used to define parts of a program that may be used in multiple places in the code, such as different modules, and may need to be modified often. For example, text strings may be placed in a header file. In this case, the translator is then able to edit the translatable strings in the header file without having to access the core code. To further aid the translator in identifying translatable text, header files can be "marked-up" so that the text for translation is easily identified. Marking up a header file is done, typically, by converting the text file into RTF format and applying styles and tags to the content that direct the translator to the translatable text while restricting access to the non-translatable text.

The principal drawback in using header files is that the translator may not be able to see and understand the context of the strings being translating. Lack of contextual information can cause numerous problems for the translator. To help avoid this situation, the translated files are inserted back into the application, the application is compiled, and then the translator can easily review the UI with full contextual information.

Resource files

Another approach to separating code from text, and one that overcomes the problem specific to header files, is to use resource files (.rc files for C++ programming) to isolate your localizable text. Resource files contain the definitions of dialog boxes, strings, and icons used in your UI. Basically, everything the user sees in your UI can be defined in the resource file, making it much easier for translators to understand the context in which the strings are used in the software.

To take this process one step further, if you isolate all of your localizable text into resource files that can be compiled into dynamic link libraries (.DLL files on MS Windows operating systems), managing multiple language localization is greatly simplified. You then have one executable file that pulls localized resources from the localized link libraries. To change languages you simply change the library files referenced by the program.

Software Localization

Web UI programming considerations

Web UI programming also benefits from techniques that separate the display text from the core code. As a developer, you have to think about how to isolate text strings that are going to be displayed on the user's screen. Unfortunately, the script languages used most commonly in Web interface development are not as structured as those used in application software development; thus making it more difficult to separate code from text. Rather than isolating text in special modules like resource files, you may have to embed your text directly in the script. To make the localization process easier, though, you can use comments to format your script files in a way that readily identifies the localized text. Then, your localization vendor can create filters that identify and "mark up" the text for translation.

Text expansion

Most languages require more characters (and/or words) to represent the same thought being expressed in English, leading to expansion of text strings. The length of text strings is important from a programming perspective and an operating system perspective.

Programming language and operating system restrictions

Now that most software development is for 32-bit or higher operating systems, string lengths are no longer very restricted, but keep in mind that string resources are limited to 255 bytes for 16-bit operating systems. If the English string is close to this limit, the translated string is most likely going to be over the limit (remember, European languages often expand by 30% or more). There are ways to create strings longer than 255 characters, but they require recoding the resources. For example, a string that exceeds 255 bytes can be moved from the resource file to the executable source code and declared as an array, each element in the array having less than 255 characters. The elements of the array are combined to create messages that can exceed 255 characters. For example, the code:

```
char gszFileExtractError [ ] =
"An error occurred while extracting or decrypting
    files from the encrypted container!"
… {a line of text for each element in the array}
"Please contact your distributor or reseller for
    a valid container for reinstall" ;
printf ("ERROR:%s", gszFileExtractError);
```

defines the array gszFileExtractError that contains a text string in each array element. The printf function then prints all of the characters from the array elements as one message—even if the message itself exceeds 255 characters (as long as the individual elements do not exceed 255 characters).

Dialog box control sizes

Text expansion also affects the design of your program's UI. A button that is sized for the word "Close" might not be big enough to fit the German translation *Schließen*. During the localization process (discussed later), buttons and menus can be redesigned to handle the expanded text. This can be avoided, though, by simply planning ahead for text expansion when designing the UI. This means that both output (displayed for the user) and input text (where a user types in characters) fields are larger than what you would normally specify for English.

Comments really do help

Comments should be used to clarify ambiguous strings by telling a linguist how many characters may be used in a string and how that string is to be used. A programmer neglecting to use comments may write:

```
#define SPS_SPOOLDIR_TITLE "Spool directory"
#define SPS_REMOTESPOOLDIR_TITLE "Remote Spool directory"
#define SPS_SETUP_DEF_FONT
 "F3FF000000000000BC020000000000030201224172696C006300
 63000007000080266F071B04B026B4A7321939070F070020"
```

Without any comments it is impossible to tell how `SPS_SETUP_DEF_FONT` is to be used. A comment detailing where and how the font definition is used makes the localization process much easier.

Number, currency, and date formats

How we display numeric data and the units that accompany such data varies by locale. Fortunately, using standard APIs today (such as those provided by Microsoft), handles much of the conversion for you as you change locale. (This is what the "region" setting is for when configuring Windows). If you are programming your own display, though, you must remember that when you localize the content, display requirements also may change. Examples of this follow below for formatting numbers, currency, and dates.

Many European languages use commas instead of decimal points and a period or space instead of a comma to indicate the thousands place. For example, the same number (5134) is represented three different ways in the US, Italy, and Sweden:

US	5,134
Italy	5.134
Sweden	5 134

Your software must support these variations or you could have a major problem when someone deposits five thousand Euro and is credited for five dollars!

Software Localization

In addition to numbering conventions, nearly every country in the world has a different symbol for their currency. Whether this symbol appears before or after the monetary amount also varies. Some examples include:

US Dollar	$ or US$
UK Pound	£
Japanese Yen	¥
European Euro	€

Date and time formats also vary from country to country. Some countries like the US use the twelve-hour clock while many European countries use a twenty-four hour clock:

US	9:35 PM
Germany	21.35
French Canada	21 h 35

Similarly, the formatting of dates varies by country. The US standard for dates is represented as month, day, year (MM/DD/YY) with various types of separators (such as "/" and "-"). The European standard is day, month, year (DD/MM/YY) with a few exceptions. The Chinese standard is year, month, day. Here are some examples:

US	January 14, 2002	1/14/2002
France	14 janvier 2002	14.1.2002
Hong Kong	2002 年 1月 14日	2002/1/14

Even determining which day is the first day of the week can vary! For example, in America the first day of the week is Sunday; however, the French calendar begins each week on Monday.

Abbreviating the days of the week should be avoided since some languages have the same first letters for all the days of the week.

Units of weights and measures

Most of the world outside of the US uses the metric system; therefore, international software must be able to handle metric measurements. Problems with units of measure are particularly acute in engineering and scientific software where rounding inaccuracies during the conversion process can have dire consequences. Great care should be taken to ensure correct conversions between English measurements and metric measurements. Remember the Mars Lander debacle that resulted in a failed Mars exploration project in 1999/2000? The difficulties with this space exploration project are rumored to result from bad conversions between English and metric measurements.

Hotkeys

Most programs have hotkeys (keyboard shortcuts) for various tasks. For example, in MS Word, pressing the Control (CTRL) and "F" keys simultaneously opens the "find" dialog box so the user can find a word or expression in the document. The hotkey CTRL+F is shorthand for using the mouse to select Edit/Find from the menu in Word.

Quite often, when translated, these hotkeys are no longer appropriate and must be changed to some key from the translated text. For example, when "Close" is translated to *Schließen* the hotkey ALT-C should change to ALT-S. The new hotkeys should be compared in the native operating system environment to ensure that all the hotkeys are unique. Interestingly, for Japanese, Korean, and Chinese, the English hotkeys are retained in parentheses after the translation!

Composite strings

One of the biggest challenges in software internationalization is coping with composite messages. Composite messages occur where two or more strings are combined to create one message. Composite messages typically have the following format:

```
"The %s has an error: %s"
```

In this composite, the %s would be replaced with the appropriate text "hard drive" and "out of space":

```
"The hard drive has an error: out of space"
```

Working with composite strings, there is no way for the translator to know the gender of the noun in the case of %s symbols.

The order of each %s cannot change unless a programmer alters the code, but the grammatical requirements of some languages might necessitate a change in word order. The contents around the variable might have to change the order in the sentence structure because of the grammar rules in the target language. If this switch occurs, and the corresponding code is not updated, then something like this sentence may result:

```
"The error is: hard drive out of space"
```

The point is made, but it is not very pretty to read!

Software Localization

One way of addressing the problem of word order during localization is to use a function to order parameters. This allows the reordering to take place in a header file instead of in the code. If you are using 32-bit Windows, word order can be fixed by using the FormatMessage() function with the %1 and %2 text parameter system, for example:

```
#define STR_ERROR "the %1 has an error %2
  …
  …
sprintf(OutBuf, FormatMessage(STR_ERROR, device, errormsg))
```

Plural constructions in composite messages

Rules for creating plural constructions differ from language to language. Even in English, the rule for constructing plural nouns is not universal: the plural for "bed" is "beds" but the plural for "leaf" is not "leafs." The following example illustrates the problem with plurals. Take the string:

```
"%d program%s searched"
```

and the string:

```
"%d file%s searched"
```

If %d is greater than one, and the %s is used to insert an "s" to form a plural construction then the message could read either:

```
"1 program searched" and "1 file searched"
```

or

```
"3 programs searched" and "3 files searched."
```

This may work for English but it won't work for the Dutch and for most other European language translations:

program	=	programma
programs	=	programma's
file	=	bestand
files	=	bestanden

In internationalizing your software, it is best to avoid these constructs all together.

Using the correct character codes

Operating systems use different methodologies for the input and output of characters. These methodologies standardize the encoding characters that represent language, so it is easy to see what characters are supported or not supported in a particular encoding. For example, US alphabet characters are supported in nearly all encodings as a subset, but "special" characters such as é, è, and all the other diacritical marks may not be.

Character sets are maps of characters used in the operating system. Some UNIX systems use a 7-bit ASCII character set that only contains 128 characters (including tabs, spaces, punctuation marks, symbols, upper and lowercase alphabetical characters, numbers, and line returns). The 7-bit ASCII character set is too limited for most foreign languages, as it does not contain special characters (such as é, å, or â). A newer standard is 8-bit or "extended" ASCII, allowing 256 characters. Microsoft Windows uses 8-bit ASCII character sets, and for UNIX computers there is an ISO standard (ISO 8859-X). The Microsoft and ISO standards are very similar.

Even with 256 characters the 8-bit ASCII does not have enough space for all the characters used by all languages. To solve this problem there are several different 8-bit ASCII character sets that contain all the characters for a group of similar languages. Japanese, Chinese, and Korean have too many characters in their language to fit in one extended ASCII character set. For these languages, 16-bit character sets (double-byte, multiple-byte, or variable-byte) are used. In an effort to simplify matters, the character encoding system called Unicode was developed. Unicode is a 16-bit code page that contains the characters for almost all languages. Unicode is now being supported on newer operating systems such as Windows NT 4.0, Windows 2000, Windows XP, and UNIX variants.

Designing for right-to-left languages

Some languages, like Arabic and Hebrew, read from right-to-left rather than left-to-right. These languages also often contain number strings and may include Roman characters that must be written left-to-right. This means there is a combination of left-to-right and right-to-left text on the same page or display. This combination is referred to as "bi-directional" text. The interfaces for these languages put menus and buttons on the opposite side of the screen: menus start on the right, scroll bars are on the left and bottom of the window, and buttons usually appear on the left side of the window. Most of this is handled by rearranging controls in the resource files, but the resources for right-to-left and left-to-right cannot be shared. Any special functions or third-party controls and software should be examined very early in the development process to ensure that they can handle right-to-left languages and bi-directional text.

Software Localization

Understanding the user's keyboard

In order to input special characters such as é, á, ō, etc., each language has a corresponding keyboard. These keyboards make it easier to type most special characters, but some characters that are used often in the US may be more difficult to enter. For example "\" in most Eastern European countries is Right ALT+Q (there is a difference between the right and left Alt keys), and several European languages like German switch the position of the "z" and "y" keys. The Japanese, Chinese, and Korean keyboards require multiple keys to be pressed to create one character. It is important to keep this in mind when choosing hotkeys, or keyboard controls.

Hard-coded characters

When writing an application, it is sometimes necessary to search for a specific character. If this character is hard-coded, a change in the code page (to support a particular language) requires a corresponding change to the source code references to the character. For example, the following code makes a direct reference to a hard-coded character:

```
/* search for specific character */
if (current = '¥')
    ProcessLine();
```

The "¥" in the original code page is replaced with " Ą " when the code page is changed to the Eastern European (Czech, Hungarian, Polish, etc.) character set. As a result, "¥" cannot be relied upon as a marker to determine when ProcessLine() should be executed. This is not a unique case, as "£" changes to " Ł " in the Eastern European character set, and "J" in the Cyrillic character set, making both unreliable markers. Hard-coded characters should be replaced with characters that can be easily redefined if there is a conflict.

Foreign sort orders

Sorting alphabetically is easy for the US and UK markets, but for other languages how do you alphabetize words with accented characters like é, ō, and à? For most European languages, the accented character is considered the same as the unaccented character and is sorted accordingly (or it follows the unaccented character). Most Scandinavian languages put their accented characters after the z (y, z, æ, å). In Norwegian and Danish, double vowels like "aa" come at the end of the alphabet. In Spanish-speaking Latin American countries "ch" is considered a single character which appears between "c" and "d." Consideration of sort order should be made at the design stage to ensure that your software functions as you intended.

Uppercase or lowercase?

In your code, you must take care when determining whether a character is uppercase or lowercase. There are several tricks you can use to determine if a character is upper or lowercase. The following code is an example of a quick way to check if a character is uppercase by determining if it is greater than or equal to "A" and less than or equal to "Z:"

```
If ( (Unknown >= 'A') && (Unknown <= 'Z') )  UpperC = TRUE;
```

While this technique works for English, the special characters found in foreign alphabets are beyond the specified range. All special characters would be found to be lowercase because they fall outside the range (even if they are uppercase). Similar problems may be encountered with tests used to determine if a character is alphanumeric or some other symbol.

From Alvaro Antunes: "This was from an episode from the TV series *Friends* in Brazil. Phoebe was presenting her plan to get rich. The second step of the plan was to open a Saturn dealership (meaning, obviously, a car dealership). However, the subtitles read something like *"Obter uma concessão em Saturno,"* which means: 'Getting a concession of Saturn (the planet).'"

Software Localization

Donald Arney
Project Manger

Donald Arney has a golden future, right? Maybe so. But the "Localization Idol" winner and his fellow finalists had to sign virtually their entire careers away to the show's producers for one shot at stardom. What happened next was even more amazing.

Double-byte enabling

It is often necessary for the program to find the length of a string. The most common technique (the function "strlen") is to count the number of bytes in a string. A byte is a group of bits (binary 1s or 0s) that are used to create a character. Most languages can be represented with a single-byte of information. Japanese, Korean, and Chinese characters, though, are represented by one or two bytes, depending upon the character being represented.

Languages that use more than one byte to represent a character create problems when counting bytes to determine the number of characters in a string. When writing programs for use in these countries, there are different functions that must be used. If you are looking for the length (number of characters) of a string then use the "`mbsXXX()`" functions. If you are looking for the size (number of bytes) of a string, then use the "`strXXX()`" functions. Remember, as well, that any strings or arrays must be of sufficient size to handle two bytes per character. For example:

```
#define MAXSTRLEN 10
#ifdef _DBCS
#define MAXCHARSIZE 2    /* two bytes per character */
#else
#define MAXCHARSIZE 1    /* single byte per character */
#endif
int    numofchar;
int    numofbytes;
char   outBuf[MAXSTRLEN * MAXCHARSIZE];
...
...
numofchar = mbslen(outBuf);
numofbytes = strlen(outBuf);
```

All functions used must be examined to see if they can handle double-byte characters.

There are other issues that should be considered for double-byte languages. Japanese and Chinese (and Thai as well, though it is a single-byte language) do not use spaces between words or characters. This can cause problems with line wrapping.

New developments in technology have made the display and input of double-byte characters much easier. With the latest Windows operating systems (Windows 95/98, Windows ME, Windows NT, Windows 2000, and Windows XP), multi-language support allows you to view double-byte characters on an English system. Of course, the application running on Windows must also support the double-byte characters, and many of them do. Perhaps the most exciting development, of late, is the support offered by Windows 2000 and Windows XP for both the input and display of double-byte characters. Finally, there are also third-party software packages that facilitate the input of double-byte text such as Richwin, Twinbridge, and NJWin.

Processing double-byte characters can present challenges. For example, some characters that you search for might be a half of the double-byte character (such as "/," "[," and "<"). File names and database fields are typically measured by "bytes" and not by the number of characters. So, a DOS file name is "8 BYTES dot 3 BYTES," not "8 characters dot 3 characters." For double-byte characters, that leaves you with "4 characters dot one character" for the file name.

Software localization

After successfully completing your software internationalization (planning for issues like text expansion, double-byte enabling, etc.), your software product is ready for localization. The localization process involves several basic steps that are applicable to all types of software projects. The details may vary, of course, depending upon the type of software being localized. Your localization vendor should work closely with you in determining the exact processes that are required for your project.

The basic steps of a software localization project include:

- Establishing a configuration management system that keeps track of each of your target language versions of source code,

- Identifying and extracting the text strings in the source language to be localized,

- Translating the extracted strings into the target language(s),

- Reinserting the translated strings into the correct source code version for the target language,

- Testing the translated software, editing the screen display as necessary to accommodate the translated text,

- Performing a linguistic review of the draft version of the localized software to ensure both form and content are correct, and

- Incorporating any final comments and finalizing the product for delivery.

Each subsection below examines the localization process for the three principal software project areas: User Interface (UI), Online Help, and Web sites.

Software Localization

User interface (UI)

No matter the programming language used or target platform (Windows, Mac or Unix), there is typically a way of isolating text strings and dialog boxes that appear on the screen. Using Microsoft C/C++ as an example, resource files (.rc) are preferably used to isolate these strings (as discussed above under Internationalization). These resource files can be compiled to create dynamic link libraries (.DLL) files for each of the target languages.

The UI localization process requires the resource files to be treated so that the linguists can easily identify those strings that require translation. There are tools available, both proprietary tools developed by localization firms and third-party tools, to assist in this string extraction process. Depending upon what tool is being used, the resource files are usually handled in one of three different ways:

- Strings are extracted from the resource files, then placed in a word processing document with pointers to their original placement in the resource file. Propriety tools often work in this way. Once the localized strings are reinserted into the resource file, the dialog boxes, menus, and graphics are modified to fit the new strings. The main advantage of this process is that the extraction and reinsertion of the text requiring localization is fully automated. On the negative side, the linguist, who is working only with the extracted strings, may not see the context in which the strings are being used.

- Resource files are treated so that text strings are highlighted to aid the linguist in identifying them in the resource file. The linguist ignores all of the "code words" in the resource file. Using this process, the linguist can see the entire resource file (though only the text strings are highlighted for editing). As a result, the context of the string can be determined—if the linguist has some experience with reading these files. The localized resource files are then modified by software engineers to edit and resize dialog boxes, menus, and graphics for the translated text. This technique is usually the easiest to implement, as the linguist requires only minimal familiarization with the resource files.

- Some third-party software programs provide a UI that displays the text strings requiring localization. The linguist works through the software package to access the UI components, translating the text strings into the target language. The software handles the reinsertion into the resource file, DLL, or executable automatically. These tools often provide graphical editors for resizing dialog boxes and buttons as the translation is performed. These systems offer, perhaps, the most linguist-friendly approach for the localization process, in that the strings and the UI are both displayed for localization and modification. Problems may arise, though, as each linguist requires an understanding of the software engineering involved and access to the localization tool. Linguists are paid to translate words, not to do engineering, so they may not be as comfortable with this approach!

Online documentation

Software packages use various forms of online documentation for user support. At the very least there is normally a "readme" or release notes file. With the advent of multimedia, software manufacturers are increasingly providing other documentation with their software. Some manufacturers have even eliminated printed materials and are relying solely on online documentation.

The two most common examples of online documentation are Help files (typically accessed through the program itself) and online manuals (for user manuals, installation guides, etc.).

Help Files

Help files are the most common form of online documentation. Microsoft has two standards for Windows Help files: the RTF based WinHelp, and the HTML based HTMLHelp. WinHelp has been used since Windows 3.0, while HTMLHelp was released in August 1997 and is becoming increasingly popular for the Windows 98, Windows 2000, Windows Me, and Windows XP operating systems. Most WinHelp files are written using tools like RoboHelp (by eHelp Corporation).

When translating Help files, the localizer needs access to the files used to build the Help:

- Source content files (.RTF, .DOC, or .HTML), containing the bulk of the Help file text,

- Project files (used to compile the Help content),

- Bitmaps or other graphics that are used in the Help files (often containing text that requires translation), and

- Other content files (such as the .CNT file used to create the table of contents for the Help file).

Software Localization

Roopa Murthy
Localization Engineer

"Localization allows us to adapt one application for many languages. It reminds me of the spirit of India—Unity in Diversity. There are several challenges though. Some are overcome by simply working with people; others require use of advanced technologies. I love both people and technology."

It is also possible to use macros in Help files. These macros should be examined to see if they work in the native operating system. For example, the following macro opens the printer's control panel:

```
ExecProgram("control.exe printers", 0)
```

When used in Windows 9X or later, nothing needs to be changed to make this work on non-English operating systems. But for Windows 3.1, the "printers" part of the macro needs to match Microsoft's translation of that section of the control panel:

```
French  ExecProgram("control.exe Imprimantes", 0)
German  ExecProgram("control.exe drucker", 0)
Dutch   ExecProgram("control.exe printers", 0)
```

Adobe Acrobat (PDF) files for online manuals

Another very popular form of online documentation uses Adobe Acrobat to create PDF files. Acrobat is a cross-platform electronic documentation distribution format, providing 100% graphic, font, and page layout fidelity on a variety of operating systems. With Acrobat, documents are viewed as the authors originally intended on virtually any computer platform. It is also possible to add functionality to a PDF file, providing hyperlinks, bookmarks, and the like to enhance the user experience.

Adobe Acrobat consists of three programs: Reader, Exchange, and Distiller. Reader allows a user to view, search, and print but not to create documents. Exchange offers the user all the features of Reader plus the ability to edit and annotate documents. Distiller allows authors to produce Acrobat documents as PDF files (Portable Document Format). A PDF file is created from PostScript printer files originally generated in some other application (such as Word, PageMaker, Quark, etc.). A PDF file can be generated from any program that can produce a PostScript file.

For a translator to be able to work with online documentation using Acrobat, they need the source files. The source file is translated and then converted into a PDF afterwards. The PDF file is then sent to the copy editor and proofreader. Using Acrobat Reader and Exchange, the copy editor and proofreader can edit the translation even if they do not own the source application.

Single source considerations

Just as single source, content management strategies have affected the documentation development world, so too have they impacted the world of online documentation. Today, it is possible to create content using a desktop publishing software package and then, with third-party software, convert this source content to Web site files and Windows Help files—all from the same source. The localization of single source content requires a hybrid approach, then, including both documentation localization and engineering localization. Typically, the source content can be localized directly and then the final file formats, be they PDF, HTML, or Help files, are "engineered" to verify compatibility on native operating systems.

Web sites

Despite the burst of the Internet "bubble" in 2001, the use of Web sites continues to grow steadily. Their importance in establishing business markets, generating sales, and hosted application services is well established. Even within an organization, the use of Web-based technologies for information management is now commonplace.

The Web has provided tremendous technological opportunities for providing timely information to your colleagues and your customers—around the world. That, in fact, is the rub: people anywhere in the world can look up your company and product information on your Web site. That information should be available to them in their own language if you rely upon them as customers (or colleagues in the case of Intranets).

It is easy to say that Web site information should be provided in your customer's native language, but there are important issues to consider before deciding to localize your Web content. Web sites, by their very nature, encourage the site hosts to update and/or modify the information frequently—visitors to the Web site expect to see up-to-date information. It is this expectation that makes localization of Web sites a bit more challenging. A change to one Web page on the site requires changes to the same page in all languages supported. Clearly, Web site maintenance becomes more complicated with each language supported.

In a Japanese hotel: "Cooles and Heates. If you want just condition of warm in your room, please control yourself."

Software Localization

Let's look at two scenarios: the Intranet for an international company and a consumer Web site for a product sold internationally. Before localizing a company-wide Intranet (with international offices) Web site, you should consider:

- How many foreign staff members use your Intranet?
- Do they require text in their native language?
- Could certain key pages be localized while leaving the bulk of the site in English?

Similarly, the decision to localize your marketing and sales pages, targeted for your specific market, should be carefully evaluated. While localizing the Web site makes your product more visible in a foreign market, you should be sure that you can anticipate a return on the localization investment. As with Intranet considerations, it may be possible to localize a subset of your pages to keep costs down while still acknowledging your global market.

Cost concerns aside, it is clear that some level of Web site localization is desirable for many businesses. The following subsections address the localization process for Web sites.

Web site localization process

The complexity of localizing a Web site falls roughly in between that of document and software localization. That is, more engineering support is required than is typically needed in document localization, but a bit less than that required for software localization.

Before localization can proceed, the Web site must be evaluated for complexity. Web pages are comprised of content (text), graphic objects, hyperlinks, and advanced engineering features. Each of these components requires consideration in the localization process. The content may be part of the page construction or dynamically loaded through scripts or a database interface.

Web text and graphics

Fortunately, most of the content of a Web page is typically text and graphics. As with the preceding discussion on documentation localization, the same rules apply. It is important to remember that HTML pages have some text that is not immediately apparent, for example:

- Page titles, that appear at the top of the browser interface,
- Graphic titles, the ALT attributes that appear when graphics are loading or when users choose not to download the graphics, and
- Hyperlink titles.

Graphic objects on a Web site that contain text are also normally localized. To avoid having to edit the graphics objects (a more complicated process than text editing), text objects should be separated from the graphic. Text can always be superimposed on a graphic using absolute positioning for graphics and text under DHTML.

Hyperlinks

Hyperlinks on a Web page have the potential to take users to regions of your Web site or to Web sites of others that are not localized. It may be necessary to modify these hyperlinks so that alternative sites are selected (if available in the appropriate language), or an explanation given in the target language that these sites are in English.

Advanced Web features

Many Web sites use features that provide more dynamic Web pages. As the pages become more dynamic, the potential for complications in localization increases. The latest trend in this regard is the interface of Web sites to content management systems that store content in XML "chunks." These chunks are then displayed on the Web site through templates that control their look and feel. Other technologies, such as the use of program scripts (CGI, Perl, Java and Active X controls) provide dynamic functionality to Web site displays and content.

As Web sites become more dynamic in nature, their functionality must be considered during the localization process. Ideally, the same standards for software internationalization are applied to any code or scripts that are included on the Web site (simplifying the localization process). As with software projects, any text strings used in the script must be identified for the localization process. Fortunately, the amount of text in these code modules is normally quite small and therefore localization is straightforward. Still, these modules must be tested on native language operating systems, to assure they function properly.

Software Localization

Steve Heikkila
Project Manager

"Hi. My name is Steve. As a member of the species anthropos, I am a zoon noumenon, sui generis, a legislating member of a kingdom of ends, and a citizen of the cosmopolis. For the life of me I cannot recall the last time we translated anything into Ancient Greek or Renaissance Latin."

The most complex addition to the Web arsenal is the database interface. It is the database that makes content management systems work effectively. Here, much of the page content is stored in a database and then displayed on the Web page as needed. For example, if a user asks to see all of the large wool shirts that you sell, your database would serve up a list on the Web page of all of the large wool shirts you have in inventory. If this list is localized, then an added level of complexity is introduced to the Web page: the database not only must serve up the list of shirts, but the right localized list of shirts, and that list must fit correctly onto the page. This is typically accomplished by designing the database to handle this added level of complexity with a "by language" table structure. Similarly, the Web style sheet is modified to handle the "by language" text expansion requirements so that the localized content looks correct on the screen.

Extended and double-byte characters on the Web

Web pages must be able to display the characters of languages from all over the world. The accented characters that are found in Western European languages (French, Spanish, Italian, German, and Portuguese) are relatively easy to display. Most personal computers support the extended ASCII character set required to represent these letters. For HTML, these special characters may be represented either by specific HTML codes or by setting the language encoding for the page. For example, an é is represented in HTML as &eacute (an acute accent over the letter e). These special codes are generated automatically if you use an HTML generator with a WYSIWYG (what you see is what you get) interface.

Localizing Web sites into Eastern and Central European languages, and into double-byte languages, is slightly more complicated as their character sets are completely different from that of the Western European languages. Fortunately, the browsers from Internet Explorer and Netscape, Version 4 and higher, support language-encoding metatags. As long as the user's PC has the appropriate language support (available as multilanguage support on Windows and Mac platforms), or the native language operating system, the extended character sets appear correctly. Both the Web pages and the browser must be configured to support the desired character set. Fonts must also be installed on the computer to view these double-byte languages. Using the HTML <META> tag element, the character encoding necessary to view a particular page can be set automatically. For example,

```
<META http-equiv="content-type" content="text/html; charset=big5">
```

indicates that the page is encoded for Traditional Chinese.

Software localization quality assurance

Validating the translation

Computers cannot currently fully process the complexities of human languages. To ensure that the software UI appears correctly on the screen and is grammatically accurate, the software text must be reviewed for correctness by a native-quality linguist. Typically the most thorough review is one that is done during or just before regression testing of the finished software.

Testing the localized application

The localization process itself should not lead to the introduction of new defects into the application. However, if the application is not fully internationalized, and code changes are required during the localization process, the potential exists to introduce new functional defects. To be sure that there are no internationalization defects in the application, the localized versions must be tested on a computer configured with the native operating system. A full regression test on newly localized applications should be considered a mandatory step. The localization service most often performs this testing, but the engineering group that constructed the application can also be involved to insure the tests are as complete as possible.

Functional testing and in-country review

Ideally, to verify that your software has been correctly localized, the final draft of the application should be tested in real-life scenarios on a native operating system. This can be done by your localization vendor or by your in-country representatives. This may involve the use of your international distributors, in-country user community, or native-quality linguists to perform the final review before your product is released to market.

What Makes a Translator

Willy van Grunsven
Co-Owner

"Being Dutch is synonymous with being innovative and adventurous. These qualities have proven to be my lifeline to sanity on one or two occasions in this industry. In Lingo's 10-year history, there have been a couple times when the story of the little boy who stopped the flood with his finger in the dike seemed very familiar. Fortunately, most of the time here it is more like the "Golden Ages" that my country had in the Middle Ages - a time of abundant opportunity and deeply felt, long-lasting relationships."

What Makes a Translator

We already learned that translation is an important part of the localization process. A good translator is essential to the overall quality of your localized product.

One of the first mistakes made by people new to the localization industry is to put any bilingual people they know to work translating their content. Time and again, a Japanese or Chinese software engineer who worked on the development of the software is tasked with translating the UI and then the help files for a project. When this happens, an immediate "red flag" should pop up in your mind: are you using the right person for the job? In developing the English source, you used technical writers and user interface specialists to ensure that the English content is correct and appropriate for the end user. Engineers should do what they do best: build things. Most engineers are not technical writers. So, if you would never consider asking your software engineer to write your user guide, why would you want to use that same engineer as a translator? Translators are highly trained professionals who know how to get the message across clearly and correctly, so that your end users can easily understand it. Choosing a translator is a matter of using the right person for the job.

Localization is not just about translation. Localization goes beyond translation, to the meaning behind the words that are used. Different cultures use different grammar and sentence structures, so straight word-for-word translations are never enough to convey understanding. Instead, the form of the source language must be replaced with the form of the target language while maintaining the original meaning and style of the source materials.

The art of translation is complex. An experienced translator can extract the essential information from the source material, including register (tone, style, formality, complexity, etc.) and carry it over to the target language translation. Quality of localization is directly linked to the translator's experience with the topic and knowledge of both the source and target languages.

Being bilingual is only the beginning. So just what makes a good translator?

A translator provides native-quality translations. Native quality means that the material, once translated, reads as though it was originally written in the target language. This usually requires the expertise of someone who was raised and educated in the target country. Of course, there are non-native translators with exceptional education, training, and experience in a specific language that are able to provide native-quality work, but it takes true talent.

A translator must have:

- Native fluency in the source language,
- A thorough understanding of the target language,
- Excellent writing skills, including a grammatical mastery of the target language and knowledge of various writing forms and styles,
- Familiarity with current terminology in the desired field (experienced translators often find it helpful to maintain extensive reference libraries),
- A working knowledge of the localization process,
- Access to appropriate tools such as up-to-date computers and multiple software applications, and
- An awareness of cultural differences and language subtleties.

Translators must have extensive education. Technical translators require additional experience in order to work in specific fields. We believe a translator should meet clearly defined minimum criteria:

- A Bachelor's or Master's degree in an appropriate field,
- Five years translation experience,
- Three years translation experience with material similar to the source material,
- Translation certifications such as those provided by the American Translators Association, and
- Demonstrated commitment to the profession through professional affiliations.

Using qualified translators is integral to the success of your localization project. Quality translators infuse your products with a professional style and clarity of content that contributes to the success of your international release.

Quality Assurance

Cristina Tacconi
QA Supervisor

"I started working at Lingo Systems as an Italian translator many years ago, but soon enough I found out where a real passion was taking me, and that was how the quest for the mistake-free localization project began...
With my team of experts, the 'quality assurance fighters,' we have developed our very own sophisticated strategies and techniques for detecting and eliminating mistakes of all sorts, even before the localized versions come to the QA Department for the final, unmerciful screening. How? Well... reading this book certainly helps, but the real secret is: we keep it fun!"

Producing Quality Products for Foreign Markets

As you already know from writing and producing your English documentation, Web sites or software, the quality of the writing and the presentation are extremely important in achieving product acceptance. How many times have you laughed over incomprehensible instructions for assembling a new bicycle for your daughter? You would hate to have someone laugh over something you or your company produced. The same quality requirements are applicable to localization. If you are going to the trouble to translate and localize your product, you want that product to meet your quality expectations.

Quality is subjective and the needs for quality vary depending upon the use of the final product. If you are creating consumer products, you may have very exacting quality standards whereas, for an in-house training course, your quality requirements may be more relaxed. When we talk about Quality Assurance (QA) with regard to localized product, we're looking at three main areas:

- Translation quality (how effectively the source content is translated into each language),

- Document production quality (whether the document conforms to the "look and feel" of the product branding for the foreign market), and

- Functional quality (whether your software, Web site, and on-screen displays function properly in the target market technical environment)

You want to hire a vendor who cares as much as you do about carefully reproducing, in different languages, what took you so much time and effort to create in the first place. When selecting a localization vendor it is important to inquire about their QA procedures. There are many translators and many translation companies on the market, but they do not all consistently maintain high quality standards for their work. Quality Assurance steps must be implemented at each stage of a project in order for a localization vendor to deliver the final product exactly as you requested.

Think quality

Even before the translation process begins, you should consider scheduling time for a localization-ready review of your source content and product(s). The purpose of this review is to identify possible issues that may affect successful localization. Many people already know about internationalizing software (preparing software so that it can be easily localized in the future). But, the concept here is to apply that same idea to all of your products, including documentation. The more thought you put into preparing your products for subsequent localization, the more likely you are to succeed in the localization effort with regard to resulting in higher quality, lower costs, and shorter timelines.

While taking QA steps to ready your product for localization is often well implemented in software development circles, it is less established in documentation development. This results in timelines that do not allow for thorough internationalization of the documentation.

To help you in preparing your documentation for localization, your localization provider should offer the opportunity to review or "clean up" your English documentation, making it more suitable for localization. An English document that is grammatically correct and free from inconsistencies in terminology, greatly facilitates the translation process. Similarly, consistent formatting (see Writing Tips) greatly improves the document localization process. Just think: a poorly formatted paragraph that requires desktop publishing correction would have to be fixed for each language if you wait until after the translation process is completed. If you review and clean up the document before translation begins, then the offending paragraph need only be repaired once!

Thinking about your quality needs and document localization issues early in the development process can only improve your final product.

Charles Johnson reports some funny translations: In Brazil, "Communications will be handled by two radio operators, who will relieve themselves every eight hours."

From a restaurant menu in Barcelona: *Callos* (Tripe) = "Guts"; *Calamares a la romana* = "Squints to the Roman." From a resume, he reads the applicant has "good writting skills."

Quality Assurance

Quality assurance steps

Language

To obtain the highest quality translations, your localization vendor should have well-documented linguist qualification procedures (and should follow them!) when hiring the linguists and the translation agencies they are using on your work. The linguists they use for your projects should be both experienced translators and familiar with your content subject matter. There are various ways of assuring this kind of competency, and no single way is the "right" way. Rather, it is important to know that your vendor considers the issue so that they can assure you of their linguists' competency. You should also consider checking the quality of your vendor's work by using in-country representatives from your company to review the work. This in-country review also allows your in-country representatives to buy into the final localized product. The in-country reviewer evaluates the specifications of your product against the cultural/linguistic elements of the relevant country. Usually this review is conducted by someone familiar with your products (such as representatives or distributors) in the target country. If at all possible, the in-country reviewer should be involved early in the project (at the glossary development stage), so that they are aware of all the terminology choices. Bringing an in-country reviewer on board at the project's start avoids costly rewording due to mere stylistic differences in the translation later in the game.

In addition to establishing an in-country reviewer to review your vendor's work, it is highly beneficial to start a project with the development of a terminology list. Even the best linguists benefit from this step to improve the quality of the translation. Before sending files out for translation, your vendor typically should request the development of a glossary or terminology list (either done by you or by your vendor upon review of your source material). This ensures that all the linguists working on the same projects are using the same technical terminology. By having a translated list of specialized terms from your product, all linguists working on the product translate those terms the same way, greatly aiding in product translation consistency. It is incredible how much more efficient the process becomes and how much time can be saved this way.

In order to ensure high quality, the linguistic phase of the project should normally include three steps:

- Translation,
- Copy editing, and
- Proofreading.

The translator is the "lead linguist" on your project and is responsible for converting the source material content into the target language. The copy editor then reviews, word for word, the translator's work, verifying the accuracy of the translation. Finally, the proofreader examines the final version for consistency and flow of the language.

While most commercial products should use a three-step linguistic process, there are cases where this is overkill. If you just need your content understood in the target language, you may be able to use translation, or translation followed by either copy editing or proofreading. This approach is particularly useful for internal documents (say, training materials for your new multinational accounting system). Your vendor's quality processes should mold to your needs so that you do not pay for quality that you do not need.

From Liv Bliss, who caught these at a large publishing house:
"It was not long, however, before he returned to Siberia. He had been born there, and was always fondest of his own parts."

"The Transcaucasian Federation was formed in 1922 on the initiative of Lenin, the communist parties and the boiling masses of Azerbaidjan, Georgia and Armenia, giving a political form to the "cohabitation of the Transcaucasian peoples, a farm that will breed peace and affection among those peoples." (Punctuation as in original.)

Quality Assurance

Visual review

Once the formal translation process has come to an end, the Quality Assurance process continues, in different forms (depending on the nature of your project).

If your project includes printed materials, the QA reviewers perform visual validation to insure that everything in the translated document matches the original English text (source document). The QA reviewer validates items such as:

- Completed translation (all items that should be translated are translated and those that should remain in the source language are not translated),
- Consistent font type, style, and size,
- Correct placement and size of graphics,
- Graphic content (making sure there is no clipping of graphic or text elements),
- Page flow and page numbering,
- Cross-references between text and the table of contents and indices, and
- Text indentation and alignment.

This list can expand considerably and is normally customized for every single project, given input from the client. To help your vendor develop quality guidelines, it is a good idea to provide them with any information that can aid the translation and QA steps early in the localization process. Some examples of helpful information to provide to your vendor include:

- Terms and names that are to remain in English,
- A list of part numbers for your products, and
- Measurement units to be used in your document (inches/mm, pounds/grams, Celsius/Fahrenheit, etc.).

Functional testing

Just as for your printed documentation, any online documentation should be validated in a QA review. The two main online documentation types today: PDF files and HTML files also require functional testing. Your localization vendor should be able to perform functional testing on your products to assure that they work the way they are intended to on the software platforms consistent with your target markets.

Both PDF files and HTML files need to be tested on computers running native operating systems to ensure that the functionality and character displays are correct. Typically, these files are checked for:

- Compatibility with native operating systems,
- Correct display of fonts and graphics,
- Compatibility with appropriate localized Acrobat Reader versions and HTML browsers,
- Correct function of hyperlinks, and
- Clear printing of pages.

This list may be customized with other items, depending upon any advanced features that may be added to the PDF or HTML files.

Renato Beninatto writes: "In Brazilian Portuguese, tooth means *dente* and teeth, *dentes*. However, several dentists must think that *dente* translates as dent in English because they name their business practices with titles like *Super Dent* and *Clinident*. There are also products, such as a chewing gum, called *Cleandent*. If only they knew that an English speaking person reading these names might think the Brazilian dental offices or products were for car body repair."

Same Language, Different Dialect

Aleks Smetana
Localization Engineer

"Born and raised in the Ukraine, I speak three languages but my real passion is programming languages. It seems pretty logical, then, that I work as a Localization Engineer in the Research & Development department of Lingo Systems. Here I can utilize both my engineering and linguistic skills, and also have fun working in a multicultural environment where I can represent Eastern Europe."

Winston Churchill once described the US and the UK as two countries separated by a common language. In translation, a similar challenge arises when writing for other languages:

- Spanish readers in Madrid versus Mexico City,
- French readers in Paris versus Montreal,
- Portuguese readers in Lisbon versus Rio, and
- Chinese readers in Beijing versus Hong Kong

Spanish

The world of technology is fast-paced. Author Alvin Toffler once said, "What was unknown yesterday is old hat tomorrow." As new technologies are implemented, new vocabulary must be invented that explains it. We have to use nouns, and sometimes verbs, in new contexts.

Throughout the world, there are approximately 300 million people who use Spanish as their native language. This fact poses an interesting challenge to the translation and localization of any material, as the language evolves in each region.

Spanish translators find the problem compounded by the fact that they must write for an audience that is found in regions on two sides of the Atlantic Ocean: Latin America and Spain. Although the differences are minimal, there are linguistic variations and peculiarities that characterize several Spanish-speaking countries, the greatest one being pronunciation.

The glue that keeps the Spanish language together as one linguistic unit is the *Real Academia de la Lengua Española* (Royal Academy of the Spanish Language). The Royal Academy sets the standards of the Spanish language for all the Spanish-speaking countries in the world. Their decisions are meticulously observed by those who teach, write, or are in any way involved with the use and implementation of the Spanish language.

Given the lasting impact of their decisions, the Royal Academy is painstakingly slow in reaching those decisions. While the arbiters of new terminology may proceed at a very slow and cautious rate, technology races along. Until the Royal Academy decides each issue, the Spanish translator is forced to make his or her own decisions on terminology. Experienced translators are always careful to use terms that are understood by the greatest number of users, regardless of their location.

If Spanish has a regulating body that decides all matters concerning written Spanish (grammar, syntax, spelling, etc.), then why do some people believe that there are different kinds of Spanish? As noted above, the greatest differences exist in the way words are spoken and the way certain letters are pronounced (or maybe not pronounced). Thus, in certain parts of Spain, the letter "z" is pronounced as a soft English "th" as in the word "thin," whereas, in Latin America the letter "z" is always pronounced as an "s" as in "Sam." However, whether in Argentina, Mexico, or Madrid, the word "*zapato*" (shoe) must always be written with a "z." Local differences can also be found in the use of certain nouns—especially those that designate agricultural products: the English say "potato," Latin America prefers "*papa*," and Spain "*patata*."

Geography can also play a role in the determination of terminology. With the geographical proximity to the United States, some Latin American countries identify more closely with terms used in the United States and "Spanish-ize" the terms. A good example is the word "computer." In most Latin American countries "computer" is rendered as "*computadora*." In Spain, because of its proximity to France, "computer" is rendered as "*ordenador*," from the French "ordinateur." That geographical proximity is not always the determining factor can be seen from another example, the English term "font." Latin America prefers "*tipo*" or "*fuente*," while Spain has kept the English word "*font*."

While these examples compare Iberian and Latin American Spanish, other linguistic differences occur within Latin America. Chile, Columbia, Argentina, and others may identify more closely with Europe than the United States, yet the rule is not hard and fast. The decimal and thousand separators are good examples. Mexico, Central America, and some South American countries use these separators in the same way as the United States (where one thousand twenty is represented 1,020.00). Chile, Columbia, and Argentina prefer the European way of expressing separators (where one thousand twenty is represented 1.020,00).

Experienced translators avoid colloquialisms and regionalisms used in specific countries. Instead, they use terms that are understood by the majority of readers.

Same Language, Different Dialect

Octavio Paz, Mexican poet and Nobel Laureate for Literature (1990), said that there is really no Cuban, Mexican, Spanish, or Argentine literature. We can take this one step further and say that there is really no Cuban, Mexican, Spanish, or Argentine Spanish. Difficulties with the language exist only to the degree of formal education and sophistication of the speaker, and, by extension, to the reader's degree of formal education and sophistication.

Portuguese

Nearly 210 million people speak Portuguese throughout the world today. However, spoken Portuguese is not homogeneous. It differs in grammar, pronunciation, and vocabulary among Portuguese speakers in Portugal and in Brazil.

Brazilian Portuguese was not only influenced by native languages such as Tupinambá, but also by the many languages spoken by African slaves. Although some Brazilian words made their way to Europe, most were only used in Brazil. Southern Brazil absorbed a large influx of immigrants of Italian, German, and Japanese descent. These linguistic groups made several contributions to the language spoken in Brazil. Portuguese in Europe, meanwhile, was influenced by the French spoken during Napoleon's occupation of Portugal.

In the twentieth century, the linguistic split between Portuguese and Brazilian increased as the result of technological innovations that required new vocabulary. Unlike the Royal Academy of the Spanish Language, there is no similar "watch dog" to condone adopting new terminology and grammar in Portuguese.

Internet World Magazine published a list in the Brazilian edition that pointed out some of the differences:

English	European Portuguese	Brazilian Portuguese
to access	*aceder*	*acessar*
default	*predefinido*	*default*
mouse	*rato*	*mouse*
screen	*ecrã*	*tela*

There are also grammatical differences and spelling variations between Portuguese and Brazilian Portuguese.

When localizing into Portuguese, keep these differences in mind. Your localization provider should distinguish between European and Brazilian Portuguese and should use native-quality speakers of the respective countries to localize your product. Although Portuguese speakers from both sides of the Atlantic are able to understand each other, not localizing properly can lead to confusion among your users.

French

Most natives of France are aware that Canadians speak French with a different accent but are quite surprised to discover variations in the written language. French people are not generally familiar with Quebecois customs or history. When Jacques Cartier explored the bay of Saint Lawrence in 1534, there were no translation dilemmas because the native Iroquois were not French speakers!

There are now more than six million French speakers in Canada, mostly located in the province of Quebec. In the past four hundred years, the French spoken in this region has evolved dramatically due to geographical proximity with English speakers. It is understandably difficult to maintain the integrity of a language in a region where nearly everyone is bilingual, and where the information you receive is almost always transmitted in two languages.

It is now common for French-speaking Canadians to use English words in their daily life. For example, *une saucepan* does not mean anything to a native of France but would be easily understood by English speakers. Another example is *"un flat"* which means "flat tire" in Canada, but not in France. Other examples abound, making it clear that terminology differences do indeed exist and must be accounted for in localization.

Many people in Quebec are striving to gain political independence from Canada, and for some of them, the decline of the French language is a big issue. Canadian philosopher Jean-Luc Gouin has written that the average college student in Quebec is almost a dunce in his own native language. Most would not go that far but nearly all would admit that the French Canadian language is a language in its own right.

What, then, should you know in deciding whether to translate solely into French or to include French Canadian? French Canadians understand any material translated in French since the written language is so similar. If simple understanding is your goal, the expense of translating specifically for that target audience may not be necessary.

Same Language, Different Dialect

However, if you want French Canadians to feel that your product has been custom-made for them, you should translate it into French Canadian. French translators should have their work copy edited by a Canadian colleague if the translation is intended for Canada to ensure "cultural sensitivity." Most of the time, the linguistic changes are minimal, but you can then be confident that your product is indeed targeted for Canada. Localizing products in French Canadian and French is, of course, done at your discretion. But what is your competitor doing?

Chinese

"Can you speak and write Chinese?" This, apparently, simple question can be answered by asking in turn "What does Chinese refer to? Do you mean Mandarin, Hakka, Cantonese, Traditional Chinese, Simplified Chinese, or…?" It seems that there is quite a bit of confusion regarding what exactly "Chinese" means in regards to both the spoken language and written language. Let's try to clear up some of this confusion.

The origin of the Chinese writing system is pictorial, dating back thousands of years. People drew pictures to express their thoughts—in short, to communicate. As you can imagine, this method of written communication was very cumbersome, making complex thoughts difficult to express. Since then, a number of reforms have been initiated to stylize and simplify the manner of writing Chinese. This, in turn, has resulted in a more uniform writing style.

Language reforms were implemented as early as the second century BC (during the Han dynasty). Of all the language reforms initiated over the past two millennia, none has had a greater impact than the one carried out by the Mainland China government since the establishment of the Peoples Republic of China (PRC) in 1949. The mid-20th century language reform simplified the characters used in the Traditional Chinese writing system by reducing the number of strokes needed to write a character. The end result was the Simplified Chinese writing system. The PRC and Singapore currently use the Simplified Chinese writing system. Hong Kong and Taiwan use the Traditional Chinese writing system (though the use of Simplified Chinese may now increase in Hong Kong following their integration into the PRC). It is generally easier for a person who knows Traditional Chinese to understand Simplified Chinese characters than a person who knows Simplified Chinese to understand Traditional Chinese characters.

Continuous efforts at language reform introduced the use of the Roman alphabet to "spell" the pronunciation of Chinese characters. The result was the standard Pin Yin spelling system that is widely used in China, Taiwan, and Singapore today.

In order for the Pin Yin spelling system to work, it must be based upon a standard spoken language. This brings us to one of the most important aspects of the language reform—the standardization of spoken Chinese. Pu Tong Hua, known as "Mandarin" in most Western countries, and Cantonese, are two of the several major dialects of spoken Chinese. Mandarin was chosen as the official Chinese spoken language because it was derived from the Beijing (i.e., Peking) dialect, taught by scholars and used by the government for nearly 1,000 years. Taiwan and Singapore also use Mandarin as their official language. Cantonese, on the other hand, is a dialect widely spoken in the southern regions of China (the Guangzhou and Hong Kong areas).

Although Mandarin is the official spoken language, it is by no means the only language that is used. For day to day conversation, many people still prefer to speak in the dialect of their respective regions. It is not uncommon to find that two people speaking two different dialects cannot communicate verbally, yet if you ask them to write down what they have said, they can communicate because of the standardization of Traditional and Simplified writing systems.

So, to answer that first question of "What is Chinese?" we see that it can be thought of as a "blanket term" for several major dialects and two major writing systems.

Country	Written Language	Spoken Language
PRC	Simplified Chinese	Mandarin
PRC Guangzhou Province	Simplified Chinese	Cantonese
PRC Hong Kong	Traditional Chinese	Cantonese
Singapore	Simplified Chinese	Mandarin
Taiwan	Traditional Chinese	Mandarin

The next time you hear the question, "Do you speak and write Chinese?" you should first think about what the term "Chinese" really means!

Same Language, Different Dialect

What about Japanese and Korean?

To Americans, Chinese, Japanese and Korean may look somewhat similar in their written format. This is because Koreans and Japanese, both, use Chinese characters to a certain extent. Koreans, for example, use Chinese characters to clarify the meaning of some words in combination with "Han-guel", the Korean alphabet based on phonetic sounds. The Japanese, on the other hand, use three different alphabets:

- Hiragana,
- Katakana, and
- Kanji (the Japanese term for Chinese characters).

The tricky part is that Koreans and Japanese use Chinese characters, but do not necessarily give them the meaning and sound used by the Chinese. This can lead to some confusion.

Japanese and Koreans have their own unique set(s) of alphabets but use some Chinese in a written form when necessary. This is why the three languages may look similar to one another when written. Yet, when spoken, the three cultures have nothing in common when it comes to communication. If you were to put the three different cultures together, they would not be able to understand each other. It would be a mistake to think Koreans could understand what the Japanese were saying and vice versa.

Despite the distinction between these three languages, there are some similarities. Chinese, Japanese, and Korean are composed of double-byte characters that require special handling by the localization team. For example, while European languages can be delivered to the client with standard text flows, Asian languages may require embedded graphics to represent the text.

Also of note is the fact that the syntax of Japanese and Korean phrases are ordered differently from English. Whereas an English sentence typically begins with the subject followed by a verb and then an object, a Japanese or Korean sentence normally begins with a subject followed by an object and ends with a verb. Another difference between these two Asian languages and English is that a thought may be represented in an Asian language as a phrase or a single "word," where the English phrase is a complete sentence.

	Japanese	Korean	Chinese
Alphabet(s) used	1) Hiragana	1) Hanguel	Chinese characters (used in different styles)
	2) Katakana	2) Han-ja (Korean term for Chinese characters)	
	3) Kanji (Japanese term for Chinese characters)		
Syntax (sentence structure)	In reverse order of English; Similar to Korean	In reverse order of English; Similar to Japanese	Similar to English

Michèle Landis writes: "On luggage I bought in the US, I found this: 'If defective, this bag will be repaired or replaced without charge. Please note that our warranty does not cover accidental damage, normal wear and tear.' Here is the French version: *Si défectueux, ce sac sera réparé ou replacé sans charge. Veuillez noter que notre garantie ne couvre pas le dégât accidentel, port normal et larme.* This does not mean anything in French and if you translate it back into English, it reads: 'If defective, this bag will be repaired or put back into place without a load. Please note that our warranty does not cover *normal wearing and crying...*'"

Typing Chinese

Ting Fan
Systems Administrator

"Like many Chinese from Hong Kong, I like to eat. I especially enjoy the variety offered in Portland's dim sum restaurants. Among my favorites are the bean curd rolls known as '*Siu Mai*,' the juicy bite-size pork spareribs, and, of course, the delicate and tasty 'chicken feet,' Despite the name, it is actually a delicious dish. You should try it. Maybe you'll like it. So, what do you want to eat today?"

Writing and Displaying Chinese Characters

Now that you know how to distinguish between spoken and written Chinese, you may be wondering how people enter Chinese characters into a computer and how those characters are displayed. After all, you are not likely to see a keyboard with all the Chinese characters as individual keys. With over 10,000 characters, that would have to be an extremely large keyboard. This may make you curious about other double-byte languages like Japanese and Korean as well. Much of the discussion below, while specific to Chinese, is also applicable to Japanese and Korean.

In order to enter Chinese characters into a computer, you need an operating system that supports Chinese input methods. This could be a native Chinese operating system, or some other operating system with built-in support (or with third-party software installed) for Chinese character input.

There are three general methods of entering Chinese characters into a computer: typing, writing, and speaking.

The input of Chinese characters by typing involves breaking down each ideogram into a series of alphanumeric characters using a set of defined rules. These rules allow you to create the characters with a standard keyboard. This process is an input method. Numerous input methods have been developed since Chinese computing was introduced. Two of the more popular input methods are Chang Jie and Pin Yin. A person using the Chang Jie method breaks down a Chinese character into alphanumeric characters. Developed in Taiwan, the Chang Jie method is the more popular method associated with Traditional Chinese writing. Pin Yin, developed in the PRC, is closely associated with Simplified Chinese. The Pin Yin method uses phonetics, breaking down a Chinese character by how it sounds (representing those sounds with the alphanumeric keyboard).

In comparing the two methods, if you were to enter the word "Chinese" (中文), with Chang Jie, you would type in [L for 中 and YK for 文], and with Pin Yin, you would type "zhong1 wen2" (where the number at the end of each "word" indicates the tone of that "word"). Despite the initial learning curve required to master the rules of the input systems, typing is the fastest and most effective means of inputting Chinese characters using today's technologies.

These input methods are supported directly by the computer operating system. Originally, it was necessary to use native operating systems to have access to these input methods or to purchase a third-party software bridge that enabled an English system to input double-byte characters. Today, various input methods are supported directly by Windows XP, even on the English version of the operating system.

Beyond these two typing methods, improvements in technology have led to new methods that do not require the mastery of the rules for input methods. For example, various companies have developed Chinese writing pads that connect directly to your computer. Users can write directly on the pad. The software recognizes the writing and displays the appropriate character on the screen.

Another means of inputting Chinese characters derives from recent advances in speech recognition technology. Users speak directly into a microphone connected to a computer. The software recognizes the phonetics of each word and displays the appropriate character.

These two, relatively new, alternative methods for the input of Chinese are not without drawbacks as the interpretation of written or spoken characters is far from perfect. Also, these methods are still generally slower than the typing methods. However, as technology continues to advance, they may one day overtake the traditional typing method and allow a more convenient way of inputting Chinese characters into the computer.

Once characters are input in a double-byte character set, they need to be displayed on the computer screen. Not so long ago, double-byte display for Chinese (Japanese and Korean as well) required the use of a native operating system for Chinese or specialized third-party software that supported the double-byte characters. Today, the latest Windows operating systems (Windows 2000 and Windows XP) support the display of double-byte characters, thus eliminating the need for specialized software or native operating systems. Furthermore, Microsoft Internet Explorer and AOL Netscape support the display of double-byte Web pages. This greatly simplifies the display of Asian double-byte characters utilizing US hardware and software.

Tullio De Raffaele saw a sign in a Tokyo Hotel that says: "Is forbidden to steal hotel towels please. If you are not a person to do such thing is please no to read notis."

A sign in a Lisbon elevator: "Do not enter the lift backward, and only when lit up."

In a Tokyo bar: "Special cocktails for the ladies with nuts."

Case Studies

Jeff Williams
Marketing Programs Manager

"I get to interact with people all over the world. This has many wonderful benefits—contacts all over the place and generally a free meal and a room in such world class hot spots like Marburg, Germany, Modena, Italy, and Bhamdoun, Lebanon. I guess Paris and London have fallen off the list of international destinations."

Typical Localization Project Case Studies

Localization projects come in all shapes, sizes, and timelines. In fact, one of the most interesting parts of the localization business is the fact that no two projects are the same. While the common denominator in localization is translation of text from one language to another, everything else about individual projects varies from one to the next.

The technical requirements of the project, coupled with the client's budget and timeline, influence the way projects are executed. There is, in fact, a delicate balance among cost, timeline, and quality that controls each project. To help you better understand the dynamics among these three factors, we have summarized four types of projects below. The descriptions below represent real projects, but the identifying details have been removed to protect the innocent!

Product: medical device for the home consumer

Situation

Acme Medical Device, Inc. recently developed a handheld device for the consumer market. The product analyzes and reports blood hormone levels to the user. Acme just finished testing the English version of the device and is preparing for a simultaneous product launch in the US, Europe, and China.

We have 12 weeks before the product is scheduled for release at a product launch meeting with overseas sales and marketing staff.

Because the product is brand new, we assist Acme in coordinating in-country review of the localization (by interfacing directly with their overseas market staff). Though 12 weeks is ample time for translation and testing, the project team must be well-organized and disciplined in executing terminology and in-country reviews of the materials.

Project scope

User Interface:	1,200 words, in XML format, for Palm OS
Help File:	5,500 words, in Word format
Quick Start Guide:	1,300 words in Quark format
User Manual:	12,000 words in FrameMaker format
Packaging materials:	500 words of packaging materials in Quark format
Testing:	Functional testing of the UI on native operating systems required.

Timeline: Eight weeks for initial product localization, two weeks for localized product testing, followed by two weeks for in-country review and change implementation.

Process

During the project scheduling and estimating process, Acme and our localization team determine that, while our standard three-step translation process is more than adequate to meet timeline and quality expectations, the in-country review process presents some risks. Acme does not have time available for the extensive "fine tuning" of the translations. However, Acme has a strong reputation for quality in their foreign markets, so the product must be easy to use.

In order to maximize the quality of the translation and stay on the agreed upon timeline, we take steps to integrate Acme's in-country review team early in the translation process. During the initial project kickoff, Acme and the Lingo Systems project team review a list of expectations with each of Acme's target language reviewers. Following our development and translation of a product terminology list, we provide the list to the reviewer, who makes suggestions on their target language terminology. Our linguists use the accepted terminology throughout the translation of the product. Following translation and testing of the UI, each target language, in-country reviewer is provided a demo of the translated product and has one week to perform a final verification of the translation. Following this final verification, the translation team has one week to make any essential changes.

The English translation, from German, of a marketing brochure for plant growing lightbulbs: "Illuminating vegetation cannot be compared to the lighting of, for example, a highroad. Solid, high impact construction, leading to few breakage. New, far-going ceramics, resistant to sodium guarantee long lifetime."

Case Studies

Product: software application

Situation

ABC Software has developed and marketed a banking software package successfully in the US for several years. They recently signed an agreement to sell the product in Latin America, so a localized version of the product release is needed right away. The product has been on the market for a while, so the product is a combination of legacy code and new modules that meet current customer needs. Content for translation is mostly isolated in resource files, though some content is still mixed with legacy code modules.

Project scope

User interface:	150 .rc files. Some content may come from legacy code (to be examined at the beginning of the project). Total word count is approximately 12,000 words.
Help files:	35,000 words in HTML Help file format
Documentation:	Leveraged from Help files using RoboHelp 2002 (providing 100% leveraging from the Help files)
Timeline:	Six weeks are available for initial localization, followed by two weeks of localized product testing.

Process

ABC cannot confirm that the UI content is isolated in .rc files. We perform a "pseudo translation" of the .rc files so that we can examine all the UI screens. This allows us to determine whether the UI content is limited to the .rc files or whether some content comes from legacy code. We insert machine translated Spanish content into the UI, then ABC provides us a built version to test for areas that are yet not translated. Following our test, we provide ABC a list of areas that were not translated by the machine translation. ABC is now able to implement minor code changes in order to externalize that text into .rc files. This initial phase takes two weeks, which is then followed by our normal localization process.

Product: heavy equipment operator manual

Situation

AAA Cranes has been producing extra-duty construction cranes and similar equipment for over 50 years. They are known in their industry as a worldwide leader in their market. For the past six years we have partnered with AAA to provide localized Operator Manuals for 15 overseas markets. Because we have been creating and maintaining translation memories (TM's) for each target language over the years, AAA's localization costs are typically 1/3 of what they would be paying without these TMs. Also, because up to 80% of a given Operator Manual's content is shared with previously written manuals, the quality and consistency of the content is exemplary.

Project scope:

A typical AAA Crane manual is written using a standardized template in FrameMaker and is between 15,000 and 25,000 words to be localized into 15 languages.

> Timeline: Because of the high leveraging across AAA Crane product documentation, we have been able to shave several weeks off the normal translation process. Depending on the amount of leveraging available, we would take between 5-7 weeks to deliver a 25,000 word manual in 15 languages.

Process

In this case, our localization process has been modified to maximize the benefits of leveraging across the various products. We begin the project by reviewing English master document in order to confirm that AAA's writers adhered to the style template. Following this review, we leverage the source text against our TM by language. These pre-translated files are then forwarded to each target language translation team. Following translation of the new text and copyediting the new and leveraged text, the files are formatted, proofread and go through our quality assurance (QA) review prior to delivery. Following delivery, we update each target language TM with the newly translated materials.

Case Studies

Product: Enterprise Resource Planning (ERP) implementation training materials

Situation

American Conglomeration Corp. recently began implementation of a global, corporate-wide ERP system. As part of the worldwide rollout, American has written training courses that teach their staff how to exploit all of the features that the system offers. To date, they have spent many months of effort and millions of dollars on the implementation. They realize that in order to maximize their return on investment, staff in each country require substantial system training.

Project scope

As is typical with ERP training material localization, the source content has been written here in the US using both MS Word and PowerPoint. The training is segmented logically in courses, to be taught in target languages over a 12 week timeframe. The total word count is estimated at 350,000 words of English Source text, but the final word count may increase or decrease somewhat because all courses have not been fully written at the project start.

Timeline: All course content is to be localized over a seven week period. Each course is targeted for two weeks of localization and is delivered to the in-country training teams one week prior to its scheduled "teach-by" date.

Process

Working with the client to balance timeline and budget with cost expectations, we determine that in order to meet these requirements, we need to adapt our normal three-step translation process. While American Conglomerate wants a high quality translation, they are eager to control budget and meet the training schedule. In order to achieve these objectives, we design a two-step translation process that functions as a virtual assembly line, delivering each course exactly one week prior to the teach-by date. Using this process, our in-house DTP & QA teams and the in-country translation teams are fed a steady stream of courses, enabling our project team to balance this large project, maximizing our efficiencies over the seven week timeline.

Conclusion

While all localization projects follow similar project process steps, each individual project presents an opportunity to adapt the localization process to precisely match desired outcomes. Each project is unique, so a "cookie-cutter" approach to localization does not work. The fundamentals, represented by the localization processes described in this book, must be malleable enough to meet the requirements for each client so that budget, timeline, and quality objectives are met.

From right here in our backyard in Portland, Oregon comes this gem: "A Public Transit Authority learned the hard way that it's no easy task to translate its Web site and pamphlet into seven languages. 'We were very naive,' said their executive director of marketing. 'This past winter, we found an automatic online translation service that we thought we could just run our Web site through. It was inexpensive. Life would be golden.' That is, until Transit officials got some test translations back and ran them by native speakers of Vietnamese, Chinese, and Russian. They discovered that, in Russian, the 'transit tracker' feature on the Web site became 'hunter chasing down wild animals' and the 'detours and rider alerts' became a 'roundabout way for a vigilant horseback rider.' Even their name was transformed to 'three meetings' in Chinese."

Translation Glossary

Translation and Localization Glossary

.BMP (BMP)

A standard bit-mapped graphics format used in Windows. Files end with .BMP extension.

.GIF (GIF)

Graphics Interchange Format. A bit-mapped graphics file format used by the World Wide Web. It features lossless data compression and is best for computer-generated (i.e., nonphotographic) images. Files end with .GIF extension.
(See also lossless.)

.h files

Header files. These are files used in programming (typically C++) to identify and define common items used throughout the program.

.JPEG (JPG)

Joint Photographic Experts Group. A lossy compression-type graphics format for color files. Can compress files to 5% of their original size with (some) loss of picture quality. Best for photographic images. Files end with .JPG extension.
(See also lossy.)

.PCX (PCX)

A graphics file format used by PC graphics applications. This widely used file format employs lossless compression. Files end with .PCX extension.

.PDF (PDF)

Portable Document File. A file format created by Adobe Acrobat, primarily for read-only use with Acrobat Reader. Can be edited with the full version of Acrobat. PDF files capture formatting and layout data from files created with another application, allowing others without that source application to view properly formatted documents via Acrobat Reader on any system supported by Acrobat Reader. Files end with .PDF extension.

.SHG files

Bitmaps with a hotspot overlay.
(See also hotspot.)

.TIFF (TIF)

Tagged Image File Format. Widely used file format for storing bit-mapped images on both PC and Macintosh platforms. Commonly used for scanned images. Files end with .TIF extension.

ActiveX

A Microsoft program development technology that allows data to be shared among different applications. Conceptually similar to Java, ActiveX has a significant presence in Web-based applications.

A-Link

A linking macro provided in WinHelp that allows jumps based on keywords rather than specific context strings. A-links do not have to be localized. A-links are never seen by the user and are used only by the help system.

BinHex

Binary hexidecimal. A widely-used encoding scheme that converts binary data into ASCII characters. BinHex encoding is especially common on MAC platforms. Files end with .HQX extension.

Bitmap

A graphic for which the color of each pixel is defined by one or more bits (1 bit for black/white, 4 bits for 16 colors, 8 bits for 256 colors, etc.).

Call out

A small text box referring to an element or feature in a graphic.

CAT

Computer Aided Translation is a broad term used to describe computer applications that automate and assists with the act of translating text from one language to another. CAT tools are highly effective in improving translation productivity and quality (e.g., Trados Workbench and associated utilities).

CMYK

Cyan Magenta Yellow Black. A color model in which all colors are described as a mixture of these four process colors. CMYK is the standard color model used in offset printing for full-color documents. Also called four-color printing.

Compiling

Converting a program written in a high-level programming language from source code into object code. Source code must be compiled before it becomes an executable program.

Translation Glossary

Computer code
The computer readable code that makes up a program. Also called object code or machine language.
(See also executable.)

Cropping
Trimming the edges of a graphic to make it fit or to remove unwanted parts.

DBE
Double-Byte Enabling. Re-engineering original source code to support the input, display, and manipulation of double-byte language character sets.

Decompiling
Opposite of compiling. Changing an application from computer code back into source code. Sometimes referred to as reverse engineering.

Dialog boxes
The rectangular windows used by a program to display information or request information in a Users Interface (UI) (Windows or Mac).

DLL
Dynamic Link Library. A file that contains executable functions or data for applications. Several DLLs come with Windows and are used by many applications, others are written for specific applications. Files end with .DLL extension.

Double-byte
A character defined with two bytes (16 bits) instead of one byte (8 bits).

Double-byte enabled
A program that can handle double-byte languages.

Double-byte languages
Languages that are coded with twice as much information for each character, such as Chinese, Japanese, and Korean.

DPI
Dots Per Inch. A common measurement of resolution, used in printing. The higher the number, the higher the resolution.

Drivers
Specialized programs that allow communication between peripherals (printers, scanners, video cards, etc.) and the computer.

Embedded graphics

A graphic is known as an embedded graphic if all the information for it is stored in a document and not in a separate file.
(See also referenced graphic.)

Executable

A program that can be run (executed) on a computer.

Functional QA

Testing (assuring the quality of) the functioning of a program.

Fuzzy logic

A logic that allows the concept of partial truth-truth values between "completely true" and "completely false." Used to create near matches instead of exact matches during searches, and in artificial intelligence programs.

G11N

See Globalization.

Globalization

Developing a product concept that is culturally neutral. It "works" as an idea anywhere in the world.

Glossary

A list of terms which includes extensive definitions and grammatical configurations.
(See also terminology list.)

HelpQA

An application distributed by SDL that assists in testing help files.

Hotspot

The part of a graphic in a hypertext document that, when clicked on, jumps to another location. Similar to a hypertext link.

HTML

Hyper Text Markup Language. A coding system used on the World Wide Web to format text and set up hyperlinks between documents. Similar to SGML.

HTMLHelp

A Microsoft standard to replace WinHelp. WinHelp is RTF based, HTMLHelp is HTML based.

Translation Glossary

David Martin
Client Manager

"Having spent the majority of my life in rural southwestern Virginia, I can personally relate to the process of internationalization and localization, which I've undergone in my transformation to Oregonian. This process has taken just over seven years, and many updates and various patches! My first experience in localization was back in 1997, when I was a project manager for a Portland-based web developer. I worked with a wonderful Mexican Spanish linguist who made his home in Ireland. Go figure!"

I18N
See Internationalization

Internationalization
The process of engineering a product so it can be localized for export to any country.

ISO
International organization for standardization. A world wide federation of national standards bodies from approximately 130 countries.

Java
A platform-independent, object oriented programming language. Java can add animation, spreadsheets, and information processing features HTML cannot provide.

Kerning
Adjusting the space between two text characters. *(See also tracking.)*

K-link
A linking macro provided in WinHelp that allows jumps based on keywords rather than specific context strings. K-links require translation.

L10N
See Localization.

Leading
Adjusting the space between two or more lines of text. Also called line spacing.

Leverage
Building current translation projects on those previously completed. Reduces the need to retranslate words and phrases previously translated. The process of using one translation for repeated sections of text.

Localization
Adapting a software, document, or Web site product to various markets or localities. This may require a variety of steps including translating user interface text, modifying formats for numbers and dates, and replacing culturally inappropriate graphics or system design.

Lossless
A term used to describe compression techniques that don't lose any data. Lossless compression techniques usually reduce the size of the compressed file up to 50% of the original file.

Lossy
A term used to describe compression techniques that lose some data or details. Commonly used with graphics and video. Lossy compression techniques can compress files to around 5% of their original size with some loss of data.

Multiterm
An application made by TRADOS to point out already translated terminology to translators.

Pixel
Picture Element. One dot on a computer screen. The smallest image-forming unit on a display screen.

Quality assurance
The process of assuring that the target document resembles the source document as closely as possible. The process can include, for example, verification of layout and graphics to confirm the document is complete.

Referenced graphic
A graphic that has been placed in a document, in which the information for the graphic is stored in a separate file, and minimal information about the graphic is stored in the document.
(See also embedded graphics.)

Resource files
Source files that contain information to be compiled into the program. They contain the parts of the application that is seen by the user. Typical file types include: .rc, .res, .bmp, .ico, .cur.

RGB
Red Green Blue. Blending these three colors allows computer monitors to display color images.
(See also CMYK.)

RoboHelp
An application made by eHelp. RoboHelp assists in writing help files using Microsoft Word.

Translation Glossary

RTF
Rich Text Format. A type of document that encodes formatting as text based tags. Can be opened as text to view the tags or converted to look like a Word document (without the tags visible). Used as a source file for WinHelp.

Scaling
Changing the size of a graphic so that no distortion occurs.

Screen shots
A graphic image of what is seen on the computer screen. Often used in user's manuals to show how an application looks on the screen. Also called "screencaps" or "screen captures."

SEA
Self Extracting Archive. A file that decompresses itself. Used on a Mac OS.

SGML
Standard Generalized Markup Language. SGML is an ISO standard for marking text files to show how they should be formatted. HTML is a specialized application of SGML rules.

Sizing
Changing the size of a graphic. Sizing can cause distortion.
(See also scaling.)

Source code
The human readable code that is compiled to make a program. Some types of source code are C++, Java, and Visual Basic.

Source file
A file containing source code that is used to compile an executable program.
(See also source code.)

String tags
Tags used in strings to mark where something will be added. For Example: "%s" = another string, "/n" = a return character, and "/t" = a tab, etc.

Strings
Groupings of characters (letters, numbers, and/or punctuation marks) that are used in programs such as error messages, button labels, etc. Often strings are enclosed in single or double quotes. Strings need to be translated if they contain text that will be seen by the user.

Terminology list

The terminology list is created as a reference for linguists (translators), and is usually specific to a project. It provides the linguists with the English source word and the target language equivalent. Terminology lists are created by the linguists and approved by the client prior to translation. A list of terms and descriptions are recommended for each specific case.
(See also glossary.)

Text expansion

The increase in the total number of characters that often occurs during translation.

TRADOS

A German company that creates translation tools. Makers of Multiterm and TRADOS Translator's Workbench.

TRADOS Translator's Workbench

An application to assist a translator by showing how similarly translated sentences were translated. This software program is used to store linguist-translated text and display it when previously translated phrases appear in a word file. Helps to assure consistency and reduce redundant work.

Translation

Translation is the process of converting text into another language. Culturally accurate translations convey the total meaning of the source material into the target language, with special attention paid to cultural nuance and style.

Unicode

A platform independent character set that attempts to unify all character sets into one 16 bit character set. Unicode is a two-byte encoding that allows for 65,536 (256 times 256) code points and includes all major alphabetic languages plus a unified Chinese, Japanese, and Korean character set.

WinHelp

Short for Windows help file. WinHelp is also the name of the application that runs Windows help files (.hlp).

Zip file

A compressed file created by the utility application PKzip or WinZip on a PC.

Resources

Resources

International Trade Administration,
Department of Commerce 202-482-2867

US Bureau of the Census, Center for International Business Research 301-457-1722

US Department of Commerce. 800-782-8872
- "A Basic Guide to Exporting"
- "National Trade Databank" (CD-ROM)   *www.commerce.gov*

Trade Information Center, International Trade Administration 800-872-8723
- Free telephone consulting with
  international trade counselors   *www.ita.doc.gov/tic*

US Chamber of Commerce International 202-659-6000
       www.uschamber.org

State of Oregon European Trade Development 503-229-5625
- Information on localization, licensing, selecting the right
  distributors, and market research.   *www.econ.state.or.us.*

British Chamber of Commerce 415 296-8645
41 Sutter Street, 303 San Francisco, CA 94104
- They have copies of the EU Standards   *www.baccsf.org*

International Business Standards 301-975-2000

Associations

American Electronics Association 800-284-4232
www.aeanet.org

American National Standards Institute (ANSI) 212-642-4900
25 West 43rd Street, 4th Floor, New York, NY 10036 *www.ansi.org*

American Society for Testing and Materials (ASTM) 610-832-9585
100 Barr Harbor Drive West Conshohocken, PA 19428-2959 *www.astm.org*

American Translators Association (ATA) 703-683-6100
225 Reinekers Lane, Suite 590 Alexandria, VA 22314 *www.atanet.org*

LISA .... 41-21-821-3210 (CH)
Localisation Industry Standards Association
7, route de Monastère CH-1173 Féchy, Switzerland *www.lisa.org*

Society for Technical Communication (STC) 703-522-4114
901 North Stuart St., #904 Arlington, VA 22203-1854 *www.stc.org*

Software Information and Industry Association 202-289-7442
1090 Vermont Avenue, NW, Sixth Floor, Washington, DC 20005 *www.siia.net*

Video Electronics Standard Association. 408-957-9270
920 Hillview Court, Suite 140 Milpitas, CA 95035 *www.vesa.org*

Resources

International Computer Societies

Austria	www.ocg.or.at
Australia	www.acs.org.au
Belgium	www.bfia.be
Brazil	www.sbc.org.br
Canada	www.cips.org
China	www.cie-china.org
Czech Republic	www.cs.cas.cz
France	www.asti.asso.fr/
Germany	www.gi-ev.de
Hungary	www.njszt.iif.hu
Hong Kong	www.hkcs.org.hk
India	www.csi-india.org
Ireland	www.ics.ie
Israel	www.iash.org.il/
Italy	www.a-i-p.it
Japan	www.ipsj.or.jp
Korea	www.kiss.or.kr/0menu4_e.html
Netherlands	www.ngi.nl
New Zealand	www.nzcs.org.nz
Norway	www.dnd.no
Philippines	www.pcs-it.org.ph/
Russia	www.ras.ru
Singapore	www.scs.org.sg
Spain	www.dit.upm.es
Switzerland	www.s-i.ch/
United Kingdom	www.bcs.org.uk

Publications

ATA Chronicle 703-683-6100
Publication of the American Translators Association   www.atanet.org

Intercom. 703-522-4114
Publication of the Society for Technical Communication   www.stc.org

Technical Communication Online 703-522-4114
Journal of the Society for Technical Communication   www.techcomm-online.org

Language International .... www.language-international.com

Latecomer's Guide to the New Europe 208-263-8178
A handy and concise pamphlet geared to firms   info@multilingual.com
interested in expanding their market into Europe

MultiLingual Computing & Technology Magazine..................... 208-263-8178
319 North First Street Sandpoint ID 83864   www.multilingual.com

Software Business 720-528-3770
7355 E. Orchard #100 Englewood, CO 80111   www.infowebcom.com/software

J@pan Inc... www.japaninc.net
Web site with useful information about doing business in Japan.

More Oops!

- A world-wide alcohol distributor concocted a fruity drink with the name Pavian to suggest French chic. Unfortunately, *Pavian* means baboon in German.

- Puffs Tissues had a bad name in Germany since *puff* is a colloquial term for whorehouse.

- Jolly Green Giant translated into Arabic as Intimidating Green Ogre.

- A sign on an automatic faucet in a restroom at the Beijing Airport reads, "Unnecessary touching."

- In a Bangkok drycleaner: "Drop your trousers here for best results."

- In a Russian newspaper: "There will be a Moscow Exhibition of Arts by 15,000 Soviet painters and sculptors. These were executed over the past two years."

- In a Tokyo hotel: "In case of earthquake, use the torch to pass yourself out."

- In a Greek hotel: "Please abuse the manageress only between 11:00 and 12:00."

- From Fabien Vais: "On a small jar of honey with lemon: 'Produce of more than one country,' and just below, 'Best before end.' No date appears anywhere."

- On the bilingual packaging of a couple of regular old-fashioned mousetraps: "Moose traps - *Trappes à souris.*"

- On a bilingual flier for a mayoral candidate: "Biographical notes - *Notes biologiques*" (biological in French).

- From Fred Fuxburger: "Bad translations are creeping into the general usage of words. When recently editing a text for a manual translated from English into German we found silicon chip translated as *Silikon-Baustein* in German. Silicon is the element that is the basis of many semiconductors; in German its name is *Silizium*. Silicone is a type of plastic material used for lubricants and even for breast implants. Silicone is translated as *Silikon* in German. And OOPS, we now have a silicon chip translated as silicone, that infamous material widely used in Hollywood and not in Silicon Valley (the translator misplaced the chip by about 290 miles.) The sad part of this story is that many young people with German as their native language would not recognize the joke anymore and think that the German name of the element is Silikon because this mistake is made so often."

Notes

Notes